ONCE UPON

—— A ——

TIME

I0153078

DR. HOWARD BERENS

KnowledgeStar

KnowledgeStar

Paperback ISBN: 979-8-218-96428-3
Hardback ISBN: 979-8-218-96429-0

PRINTED IN THE UNITED STATES OF AMERICA

*To my beloved partner Karen
and my kids Jessie and Dylan, the most
beautiful gifts life ever bestowed upon me.*

IN THE BEGINNING

Once upon a time, when I was a skinny twelve-year-old boy, I foolishly ran into a busy Brooklyn street to stop a high-arching pink rubber ball from becoming a stickball homerun. It all happened near my home at West 4th Street and Quentin Road intersection on a late summer day when the sun held the darkness at bay well past my usual dinner time. I believed I had just enough time to make the "Willie Mays Grab" and jump out of the crushing path of the oncoming vehicles.

It was a contest between being hit by the oncoming traffic or catching the hit and winning the game before the Brooklyn mothers and Bubbies -- Jewish Grandmothers – began their "Come home for dinner" siren calls from their open windows and fire escapes. I wanted to be the best stickball outfielder in my neighborhood. I saw the truck out of the corner of my eye. I heard the loud honk of the warning horn. I was mesmerized by the ball as gravity pulled it toward my hands. It was the first time I consciously knew that "greatness" was within my reach, and I was damned if I would give up now.

I held my waiting hands high in silent prayer as the three other players started to yell, "Watch out!" "You're crazy!" "Look out."

My focus was only pink, only round, a falling star that slowly descended towards my hands as the noisy street traffic faded onto a distant planet. I was alone; nothing existed except the ball and my small begging hands. Then, in an instant, the ball and my hands became one. Suddenly, I was aware of the "where" and the "when" and leaped back into the safety of the side street, feeling the rushing wind of the truck passing within a few feet of my triumphant moment of greatness.

It was a premonition of the rest of my life. Taking chances like that will dot the landscape of my life many times in my unimagined future. I will take them again and again without hesitation.

My life, like yours, is the result of tens of thousands of these conscious and unconscious decisions and the consequences that follow. My training as a psychiatrist has enabled me to help other people understand why they make their decisions. Understanding the "why" of a decision allows you to discover who you are and make more conscious, often more successful decisions.

Eighty-five years worth of decisions later – trying to figure out the actual number makes me verklempt[1] – I decided to look back at my choices and analyze my behavior as the observer this time.

I decided to come to myself as the patient.

This book chronicles many critical, life-changing, transformative moments that propelled me through my life. Looking back at those moments, it's unclear whether I made them consciously or unconsciously. The point is to understand better the inner voices that were heard and unheard, which prompted me to choose one path over another. I will help you learn to listen to those inner voices more clearly.

This book will permit you to step on the brakes, slow down your life, and help you look at the decisions that led you to

---

1 Yiddish; overcome, perhaps even choked up, or clenched with emotion.

this point and discover why you made those decisions. You will be able to make future choices more consciously. You can stop careening from one unconscious choice to another, feeling that you are living your life out of control, without purpose or joy, and never knowing "why" you're here.

HARVEY

My life would have turned out entirely differently had I not met Harvey. He was the most unlikely friend and teacher I could have imagined. I was in PS 177 in Brooklyn. If you're not a New Yorker, the PS stands for Public School, a middle school before High School. By the time Harvey and I reached PS 177, he was already part nerd, part bookworm, and part mad scientist. He was the opposite of me. I was content to be a happy-go-lucky slacker, underachiever, and goof-off. I was all about sports, playing stickball, goofing off as much as possible, and girls. In Harvey's world, there were no sports, no goofing off, no stickball. And did I mention no girls? Just a love of science.

Until I met Harvey, I didn't care much about school or learning. My grades reflected my being an average - okay, maybe below average - student. As far as my teachers were concerned, PS meant "Poor Student." My brilliant self was hiding behind an average student - okay, already, maybe below average - who couldn't stop talking in class. I didn't know it at first, but some part of me wanted to be friends with Harvey because that part of me was Harvey. A part of my brain had been waiting for a friend like Harvey to ignite a love of learning. It reminds me of something the great Irish poet William Butler Yeats wrote: "Education is not the filling of a pail, but the lighting of a fire." And Harvey lit that fire.

I found myself with Harvey as my teacher, diving into the things we could do that focused on science. At first, we discovered small experiments in his boxed science kit. Then we started adding chemicals and test tubes, a small low-power microscope and went far beyond the set packaged for kids. When he wore his safety goggles, Harvey looked like a Mad Scientist. It created a veritable tsunami of ideas and thoughts that significantly changed my attitude about school.

I suddenly blossomed as a student and started devouring information about biology, biochemistry, cell structures, anatomy, physiology, and anything and everything science. My grades shot up, and after passing the very tough admission test, Stuyvesant High School became my next choice. Stuyvesant is a science school with only a four percent acceptance rate for students who take the test. They get fewer applicants than Harvard, Stanford, or M.I.T. From Stuyvesant, Albert Einstein School of Medicine, one of the most outstanding medical schools in the country, started my medical education. I went from being a mediocre student to a straight "A" student, thanks to Harvey for lighting that fire that still burns brightly today. My friendship with him started me on the path of being a lifelong learner that led out of the closed culture of Brooklyn – where I probably would have become a professional stickball player – to being a prominent Doctor, Psychiatrist, and ultimately better husband and father.

ADDIE

Growing up, I was a shy kid, an only kid without brothers or sisters, and was far more interested in science than girls. Early in my medical training, I had my first serious relationship. Even though we did not get married, this relationship would create the pattern that would dictate the arc of three of my following four marriages.

I was in the student lounge taking a break from my premed studies at Brooklyn College. I saw two women sitting on a couch. One was dark-haired, and the other was very blonde. They were both attractive, just not in the same way.

I asked a friend if she knew the women sitting together in the corner of the lounge. She assumed it was the blonde and started to tell me her name. I stopped her because I was more interested in the other one. So I went over and introduced myself. She said her name was Addie. I am trying to remember what I said, but it worked. She accepted my offer to go out for a cup of coffee. That was the start of my first real relationship that lasted four years, from pre-med to the first two years in medical school.

Over coffee, I found out she was Italian. It felt like a beautiful adventure as I learned more about her. As we talked, I knew she was a bright, kind-hearted, good person. And did I mention she was Italian? Now, I asked myself a question. Why was I so much more attracted to Addie than anyone else I met until then? Looking back now, I don't know.

How she looked at me and responded pulled me deeper into our relationship. We would get together and have these wonderful and meaningful conversations. She was a good listener but always had her point of view. We agreed with each other almost all the time. She made me feel safe and at ease.

She was also strong. Not physically but emotionally. She knew who she was. She could take care of herself no matter what the challenges were. Her self-reliance made me feel less afraid to be with her. Unlike my mother, Addie did not feel the constant need to be rescued. She respected and deeply cared about me from the start until the end of our four years together. We came very close to getting married. We decided it would be a good idea and went to get blood work and a marriage license. But that's not how the story ends.

There was a horrible night when I told her we had to break up. After we spoke, I sat in the car downstairs until 5 a.m., thinking about it and looking up at her window. Her light was still on until I left. I believed there was nothing else we could do. I was too young; I wish I was older, had finished medical school and an Internship, and had more experience. Perhaps the story would have a different ending.

By that time, I was a second-year medical student. In my mind, I imagined myself being married, trapped as a General Practitioner somewhere in Brooklyn, raising kids, and not exploring and discovering the world or myself. It felt so rigid and pre-planned. My fears about being caged in a predefined role, about being suffocated, were stronger than my sense that Addie would be supportive. On some level, she would be open to me growing and discovering more about myself and the world of medicine. Still, I could not see myself getting married at twenty-five. I know our breakup hurt each of us deeply. I had good reasons at the time. We came close to a life together, but I needed to move on.

Addie and my mother came to the airport to see me off to Israel and London for six months of study abroad. I remember hugging them both goodbye, turning, and boarding the plane. It was a final goodbye for me and Addie. At the time, I didn't appreciate the magnitude of such a decision. I never looked out the window and never looked back. I was too excited to be heading into my first real learning experience with real doctors and the reality of my medical future. Even then, I knew no matter what shape the relationship took, we would be, and are, to this day, friends for the rest of our lives.

WHEN THE MAFIA DARKENS YOUR DOORSTEP

My trip abroad during my senior year at medical school began with my time abroad shadowing foreign doctors. My first stop was in Israel, a big waste of time. The Israeli doctors would only speak Hebrew, a language I did not know and were more focused on having an American doctor move to Israel than teaching me anything about being a doctor. So, I then went to London, hoping my education would continue.

It was a typical bone-chilling cold rainy night. I was at my temporary home studying in the small apartment I inherited from another med school student when the phone on the bedside table started its English jangling that I had not yet become accustomed to. My mother called long distance; charges, of course, reversed. It had to be very important.

She was verging on sounding hysterical, telling me there had been a knock on the door, and when she opened it to see who it was, she was staring into Vinny's red face. Vinny was the local Mafia Loan Shark. He had brought Vinny Junior along to add more muscle to the visit. They had come to collect their money from Bob, who I am ashamed to admit was my deeply depressed, always-in-debt incompetent father.

My mother told me she tried to slam the door, but Vinny and her son pushed back harder, and after some pushing and pulling, my mother lost.

"They shoved past me without a word, almost knocking me down," she told me, almost in tears.

Vinny and Junior quickly marched into the dining room, where my father was forever bent over his illuminated magnifying glass, looking at different magazines in the leather industry.

"Howie, I was so afraid there would be blood everywhere," she added.

Well, maybe not ``*everywhere*" or even "*anywhere,*" but that's how my mother was hysterically describing the scene.

Lill said she quickly grabbed the phone off the wall, called my Uncle Sydney, Bob's younger and bigger brother, and started yelling, "Sydney, Sydney, help. Vinny's going to kill Bob!"

Sydney worked close to their apartment and knew Bob was living on borrowed time and money from Vinny. When he heard Lill screaming for help, he raced over. The door was still open, and he charged through. According to my mother, Vincent Junior heard him coming, wheeled around, and threw wild punches at Sydney's face.

Vinny Senior grabbed Bob by the collar and hit him on the head, yelling, "I want my money. I want my money. And I want it now!".

According to my mother, Lill, Bob finally jumped up and started wrestling with Vinny. Sydney and Vinny Junior danced together, locked in a bear hug. The fighting continued for a while – Lill said it seemed like forever – and then suddenly stopped. They all stood there, disheveled and panting, looking at each other. Then they all laughed as if they were schoolboys caught by the principal roughhousing after the recess bell went off.

After they stopped laughing, Lill told me Sydney asked Vinny, "So how much does Bob owe." Vinny spits out a number that Lill said almost made her pass out. She had no idea Bob owed so much. Without hesitation, Sydney, who was not wealthy, took out his checkbook and wrote a check for nearly eight grand. Sydney handed Vinny the money and asked if that was that. Vinny said yes, and then he and Vinny Junior left through the open door without a word. The whole story made me feel embarrassed, sad and disgusted that my father was such a loser that my uncle needed to take care of him.

That's when Lill told me the fireworks went off. Sydney started yelling at Bob, telling him to wake up. He kept yelling at his brother to get a real job and stop with the magazine craziness. Lill said Bob kept defending the magazine dreams that had him huddled over the living room table for over a year. Sydney kept yelling, "Get a job. You can't live off Vinny's money forever." Bob finally seemed to open his eyes and wake up. He told Sydney he would get serious and find a job.

Lill told me that after the confrontation with his brother, my father got a job with the insurance pharmaceutical company with the help of his youngest brother, Bernie, who worked there. It was a surprise and a relief. He happily delivered drugs to different pharmacies, restocking their supply from his new company. Later on another call, my mother proudly informed me that he takes her around to all the drug stores on his route, and she helps him sort out the packages for the next stop.

Sydney was holding up a mirror to him. Fortunately, it finally forced Bob to look hard at who he was and how it affected everyone around him. According to Lill, it was a wake-up call. It was as if he snapped out of a dream and finally got moving. As Lill's call went on, my anger quickly grew into rage. I didn't want this person as my father.

I thought of him as a black hole sucking the energy out of the people he depended on. I had my problems and didn't need this situation with my father's depression and his get-rich-quick fantasies. For the rest of my life, I would always be very concerned about earning money and being self-reliant and independent. It would even become a focus for my children later in my life. I would never feel safe and secure until they were successfully employed.

After she hung up, I was glad Lill called. I realized the whole thing was a turning point for Bob and me. I thought my father was a loser. He was severely depressed and unable to even look for a job, spending endless hours bent over at the dining room table, hiding from the reality of his situation, working on countless designs for a trade magazine that would never be published. He was lost, imagining he would be a big hit and make a lot of money. It was a waste of time supported by the money Vinny loaned him.

I knew his relationship with his father was traumatic, and he felt demeaned and often rejected. I felt sad to know how damaged he was. Yet I was so angry at my father that I almost wished Vinny had hurt him. I thought he deserved the confrontation with Vinny for his total lack of a sense of responsibility to his family. My mother and I suffered daily, worrying about how they would get by. I hated the mess he created without any apparent guilt or sense of empathy for her or me. To this day, I still find it hard to have any compassion for him. I wish I did. Without mercy or forgiveness, anger is one of the most painful emotions I've felt in my entire life.

When Albert Einstein Medical School accepted me, Bob didn't even have a penny towards the two thousand dollars for the admission. That was covered secretly by Julius, my grandfather. Julius never let me know that he had sent the tuition.

I just showed up at Einstein, and they told me to go to my room at the dorm. I learned the actual story years later. Julius did it because he was so proud that I was going to one of the best medical schools in the country. I never had the chance to thank Julius, and I never had the opportunity to let my father know that I finally understood why rejection, failure, and pain were such deep emotions in his life.

During my six months abroad in my senior year of medical school, I sat in dreary London, facing my upcoming Internship in Wisconsin, having learned almost nothing from the doctors I followed around every day. My senior year had yet to prepare me for what came next.

Internships are challenging, and you have a vast set of unique challenges and expectations with each new patient. You are expected to be a real doctor and know how to heal sick people when they come to you for help. I wasn't ready. I was scared for the first time in my life. I just knew that I would work hard and do a great job. I consciously decided to become the best Doctor I could be, which drove me through medical school and beyond.

MAKING IT REAL

After six months of learning nothing in Israel except some Hebrew phrases and then in London, where I knew very little about doctoring, I finally graduated from Albert Einstein Medical School. I had a lot of book knowledge but hardly any know-how from my six months abroad. I was looking forward to learning from real doctors, handling real cases, and working in a real hospital environment. I decided to do my one-year Internship in Medicine, Surgery, Dermatology, and ER at the University Hospital in Madison, Wisconsin, and the Milwaukee County Hospital Emergency Room. It was 1968, and I was ready to take on the challenges of being a doctor first and then as a psychiatrist.

FEMALE MEDICINE

My Internship started with three months of female medicine. Pierre Ferozen was the senior resident in the female ward where my Internship began. The environment was focused on helping each other learn. I was fortunate to have him as a tutor. Pierre was happy with me and my can-do attitude, and I was devoted to learning all I could. I was a hardworking student who took in as much as my often-exhausted self could. I was obsessive and driven to comprehend how the human body worked. I was in awe of the enormous complexity. How can we have such phenomenal complexity that works? And I had not yet begun to study the human mind,

The Internship is the most critical part of becoming a doctor. Internships take an entire year, focusing on medicine. After spending countless hours with medical books and classes and acquiring the basics in medical school, it's a beautiful feeling to begin understanding the workings of the human body. The mind would come later. My Internship was when I learned what to do when the miraculous body did not work.

Pierre was an excellent medical resident who sat down with me and reviewed each case in detail. We talked about what I should be observing, what I should be thinking about, and what the differential diagnosis is. He was precise and knowledgeable and helped me learn which tests I would need to order and how to interpret the results. Pierre taught me to ensure the patient was seen, heard, and cared for and to watch for sudden changes. Most importantly, I was learning that the patient wouldn't just be passively waiting around for the Doctor and saying okay to anything I said.

Pierre made sure that I knew everything the books said about the disease. He patiently waited for me to be confident I understood the mechanism and the underlying principles of the patient's illness and which medicines would help. Pierre wanted me to know all the basics. Since I had a good background at Albert Einstein Medical College, my diagnosis was grounded in my understanding of Biochemistry, Physiology, Anatomy, and more. All that knowledge fed into my growing know-how ability and paid off.

So, I caught on quickly when Pierre confronted me to think about this person's actual or possible disease. After rounds and seeing patients, I would return to my apartment and study the books about the diseases we encountered. Between rounds with Pierre and studying to learn all I could, I was busy twenty-four-seven, day and night. I don't know how much sleep I got, but I made sure I could describe what was happening with the patient the following day when I returned to the hospital. I could tell Pierre what I had learned.

He was fantastic, telling me when I was right on target or not. That was extremely important to me as a young intern. Once I had that understanding of one patient and the next, and the next, I was adding to my storehouse of knowledge and know-how. I was learning "doctoring," and I was doing it in a way that would help me become a real doctor.

One of the critical lessons I learned while interning with Pierre on women's medicine is that science and medicine are constantly advancing. Many of the patients I saw made me realize that it is imperative that I knew and took advantage of the most recent research and the experience of all the doctors. I was not shy about talking with the other interns or to doctors in the hallway and asking what would cause a patient's illness. It was essential to know what was in the current literature, what they could refer me to, and their experience. I ensured I understood this case and this patient with the most up-to-date knowledge I could find.

I was very conscientious and diligent, which made me feel much better about myself and my path in life. I played a central role in helping people who were sick and needed help. I cared about how they felt, helping to cure them, and made it a point to be available when they needed me. At this point, even though I had no time to find out what my choice to be a psychiatrist would mean, my work and learning set the stage to be a good doctor for my current and future patients.

MALE MEDICINE

After three months with Pierre in female medicine, I had three more with Murry Epstein in male medicine. He did the same thing. He made me think about the dynamics, the differential diagnosis, and all the things critical to gaining a deeper understanding of the patient and disease.

By the time I had six months under my belt, I felt like I was finally starting to feel like a real doctor. It was the second time I was lucky to have another outstanding resident to help me. Murray was brilliant, and fortunately, he loved to teach. I learned an incredible amount about doctoring from my time with Pierre. Still, Murray fine-tuned my knowledge even more. I loved the support and the challenge. In three more months, I became even better at working with patients and could trust my knowledge more than ever. Murray fine-tuned my thinking and understanding of how our bodies worked and why they failed and became diseased.

In discussions with other interns, it was clear how good my knowledge was. If I had done a different six months instead of Israel and London, I'd have been less panicked, but those two men saved me and helped my few patients. I loved that time with both of them. It was the most challenging and rewarding time I've ever experienced. I was lucky to have these two men as my residents who valued teaching me what I needed to learn.

At this point in my training, the most significant difference was that I asked better questions. I knew a lot more than I did in the beginning. In only six months, I felt extremely confident that I knew my medicine and could talk to other staff members about a case, and they would listen. I could intelligently discuss my understanding of the disease, potential diagnosis, and anticipated treatment. It was not like I was starting from scratch. I could look at myself and think I was succeeding at something complicated and challenging.

IT'S ONLY SURGERY

After a three-month rotation in male medicine with Murray, the next rotation was surgery. Like many surgeons, the senior resident only wanted to do surgery. Surgeons must understand the underlying medical, physiological, and organ dynamics before they begin an operation. The senior resident was happy to have me do all the pre-surgical workups and give him the correct evaluation before using the scalpel.

During the surgical rotation, I was in charge of working up every patient scheduled for surgery. My job was to check out the patients and ensure they were ready. I was responsible for the pre-op workup, providing that the medical diagnosis was correct, what the problems the surgeon might encounter, and warning him to deal with a problem or giving him the okay to go ahead. I had to check that they did not have an underlying condition that the surgeon needed to know about and make the decision not to perform the surgery or take an entirely different approach.

I took care of all the medical issues that were present for that patient. I made careful notes about everything the surgeon needed to know, anything I noticed, or something requiring a discussion. I wanted to make sure the surgery was performed without any surprises.

I handled all the pre-op medical parts during those three months of surgery. It was a lot of responsibility but an excellent opportunity to learn more about medicine. I completed complicated medical evaluations, said yes or no to a surgical procedure, and told the surgeon, considered a god in the pantheon of doctors, what the surgery required. My understanding of medicine was increasing exponentially.

I didn't focus that much on the actual surgery. On a couple of occasions, I assisted in appendectomies. I could experience the principles behind an operation and the simple surgical techniques involved. The life of a doctor is full of surprises, and you never know when you might have to do an emergency appendectomy.

I could make a diagnosis on my own. I could evaluate relevant specifics about the patient and get up to speed on an accurate diagnosis. I could quickly double-check the right books for any additional knowledge about the disease and cure.

I found this quite remarkable. By spending three-quarters of a year of intense involvement with the medical process from diagnosis to treatment, having 100 patients, I realized I could understand the pathology and treatment of a disease. It was a remarkable change in my sense of myself as a capable and effective doctor. Nine months into my residency, you could call me "Doc," and I would answer, knowing what I was talking about.

From an emotional point of view, I had crossed a line. I was finally no longer afraid of not meeting the expectations of the role I had chosen to take in life. I felt liberated. Ultimately, my love of learning was helping me feel successful, replacing the family history that always brought me down. My conscious decision to make sure I was good and competent had driven me to this point. I was free of the grip of my past and ready to take off and fly. I felt delighted helping people who depended upon me and were there for them.

YIKES! THE EMERGENCY ROOM

After three months of surgery and six months of female and male medicine, I picked one month in the Milwaukee County Emergency Room. I could have chosen an easier rotation, but I was out to prove I could handle myself under the most challenging conditions. The ER is a demanding litmus test for a new doctor. And "new doctor" was now how I described myself.

The ER was a stressful situation. I was the only one on call at night, the only physician you'll see when you have an emergency. The ambulance picks you up, takes you to the hospital, and you get me, Doctor Berens.

Most doctors, especially residents, learn early in their training to work together and cooperate on cases. If something was over my head, I would still respond to the situation because somebody was always on call, from surgery to neurosurgery and the other branches of medicine. I would do a workup on the patient, wait up to three hours for the lab results, and then ask for help. I always asked for help with complicated cases that had to be taken into surgery immediately. It was the reason they called it an ER.

One moment stands out when my experience and ability to make decisions saved a patient's life. Four large policemen carried a man into the emergency room, each holding an arm and leg. The man was crazily thrashing around, screaming and yelling at the top of his lungs. They brought him to me, slapped him down on a gurney, and said the guy was having a seizure and was utterly crazy.

I looked closely and carefully as the police held him down on the gurney. I quickly grabbed a vial of sugar water, gave him an injection, and waited. The injection was the equivalent of a sugar cube. I did it without saying a word. Just motioned to the police to hold his arm down, tied it off, got a vein, and gave him the shot. What happened next was what I expected. He was a diabetic and experiencing a diabetic type of response. The injection was the equivalent of a sugar cube. The man calmed down almost immediately, opened his eyes, stopped thrashing, and said, "What am I doing here?"

I told him he probably had his insulin that morning but had nothing to eat with sugar all day. I told him to go home, eat a candy bar, and call his Doctor. He thought about it briefly and then told me it had happened before. When he sat up, the four policemen looked at each other and then at me.

I was so glad I knew what I was doing then, and it was crucial when I gave the patient the sugar injection. He had diabetes, and I knew it, so I was not scared to use the glucose. It felt great to be the Doctor in charge, helping the patient and impressing the police officers.

What was wrong and what had to be done became evident to me. But it had taken incredible hard work, dedication, and perseverance to get to this point when I knew what I was seeing and what to do. I was proud to be the Doctor, the caregiver everyone turned to for help.

Working with the person with diabetes was one of the most critical turning points in my growth as a person and a doctor.

Looking back, it was so powerful that it was more important than many other moments of success and triumph. I ensured that the right thing was done at the right time when I cared for others.

SKIN DEEP

I had two more electives to pick from, and after the pressures in the ER, I wanted a break, so I chose dermatology for one month, thinking it would be the easiest. I thought dermatology would be a throwaway course, but it was valuable. I learned a lot, and the doctors always tried to teach me as much as I could absorb. I learned about tropical medicine and the many diseases of the skin I would have never imagined. Seeing people worldwide come in with a rarely seen tropical disease was like living in a dermatology lab. Every day was a new case to study and from which to learn.

Dermatology was, in many ways, more manageable than the other rotations because it was rarely life-threatening. The residents who were on this service at the same time were a little more low-key, but I still learned a lot. Dermatology is genuinely a significant branch of medicine. When I made rounds of the thirty or so patients hospitalized or in the outpatient clinic, my team diagnosed some very esoteric diseases, many from other parts of the world. Not bad for an area I initially thought would be a waste of time.

THE PROFOUND JOURNEY

Psychiatry has always been my fascination and focus since I started medical school. I quickly learned that medicine is very different from psychiatry. Some psychiatric insights are so invisible and hidden that they are not apparent until a powerful event brings them to the surface.

During my medical Internship, I had some profound insights that were significant and very different from my success with the patient lost in an insulin storm. That injection was concrete. I recognized the problem and quickly found the answer. Psychiatric illness is often more elusive. Both require the same kind of dedication, perseverance, and learning. My life's goal was always to ensure I gave it all I could, even if flying solo.

But as this difference became more apparent to me, I realized that my knowledge of medicine had yet to turn to psychiatry entirely. I enjoyed the medical aspects of doctoring, the mastery of female and male medicine, surgery, and emergency room medicine. Even learning about dermatology was a profound psychological journey, setting me free from my family's dysfunction. If medicine did that much, I wondered what psychiatry could do.

The entire course of my Internship so far had no psychiatric rotation. Studying medicine had practically cured my toxic negative self-image and emotions about myself created by my father and, to a lesser extent, my mother. That is what happened as I became an excellent and competent doctor. I worked out the deeper source of my pain and anger that had been getting in the way. The hard lessons I learned and the fears I overcame as a doctor helped me grow significantly.

So far, this was the first step. Since I started studying, psychiatry has always been on my mind as the ultimate goal I wanted to reach. At that point, after my Internship in medicine, I knew that psychiatry would be the journey into my soul. *It would be as mysterious as a religious experience.* I believed, hoped, and trusted that the process would enable me to face my deepest fears and discover my authentic self. And I was more than ready to pay the price if that was what I needed to do. I had no idea then that I would become my own patient one day.

My choice and feelings about going into this field probably had much to do with the trauma I witnessed in my family. I swore that the insights and self-awareness I would gain would help me never regress and never go backward to where I was at the start of my training. I would be fearless and open to new ideas and approaches, contributing to the happiness and self-development of other people's lives.

The initial focus was on medicine, what could go wrong with the body, and studying each organ to learn how they functioned when normal and diseased. It had an excellent education and foundation for what came next.

Now that I was well-versed in the workings of the body, I was ready to look into the mind and become a Psychiatrist. It was time to start the journey that would last the rest of my life.

It was fate that Psychiatry's one-month rotation put me directly in the path of Carl Alanson Whitaker, a famous psychiatrist and unorthodox family therapist. He was a visiting professor on my ward doing family therapy during my elective rotation. He was demonstrating his very unique approach to family dynamics.

I sat next to him during one of his demonstration sessions. At one point, I raised my hand to ask a question. Carl turned and hit me on the shoulder, telling me in no uncertain terms, "This is my session." I could still feel that punch as I started my three-year residency in Psychiatry at Boston State Hospital.

FREUD AND ME

The 3-year psychiatry residency began at Boston University Medical Center. The first year, I had a small number of in-patients and two middle-aged male supervisors who worked with me on my treatment of patients admitted to the ward. Some remained for as little as a few weeks, and a few stayed for several months. I saw them weekly and had my supervision on a regular daily schedule.

They focused on teaching me Freudian concepts in each case and how I might do therapy with them. At that stage, I did not know enough to fully understand what they were doing, so they emphasized helping me learn. Their focus was entirely on intensive one-to-one treatment and psychoanalytic theory.

As I imagine you already know, psychoanalysis is a Freudian approach to psychotherapy. This approach is designed to uncover unconscious motivations. From one perspective, it places the therapist as the all-knowing savior, leading the mentally challenged out of their confusion and pain.

In the first week of my psychiatry residency, an internist called me to the ER, saying he had a patient being referred to the psych department. I completed my Emergency Room medicine internship and was qualified to attend ER patients. This patient was a black man in his 50s. Since he was slightly disheveled and incoherent, the intern assumed the patient was mentally ill and should be admitted as a psychiatric patient.

When the intern left, I spent 45 minutes evaluating the patient medically and neurologically. I found out that he had lost a sensation from the belly button-down. I used a pinprick and stuck it into his skin below and above the belly button. He had normal sensation above but no sensation below at all. This probably meant he had a spinal tumor in Thoracic 12 that cut off feeling from all nerves coming in from below T12.

So, I drew a picture of my diagnosis in the chart. I also wrote my diagnosis and the evidence for my diagnosis in great detail. I told the medical resident to come back down, and he returned. The nurses were giggling in the background, thrilled to see him about to be embarrassed for missing the diagnosis because they thought he was an arrogant know-it-all.

I showed him the chart, and he read it and said, "Oh boy, I got one-upped by a shrink. I must say you guys aren't complete idiots. You know your medicine." I got applause from the nurses, and the patient went to surgery that night, and they found a tumor exactly where I said it was. Fortunately, it was benign, cutting off nerve sensation as I had diagnosed. I got an apology from the medical resident. I told him I've just been well-trained; that's all I can say.

Even the surgery department was impressed since they found a benign tumor exactly where I had said it should be. I was very proud of what I had done, and the following day, as people came to work in the hospital, almost everyone had heard the story about a psychiatrist figuring out a complex medical problem. The entire psychiatry department was vindicated, and everyone praised me. It demonstrated that psychiatrists knew their medicine. The next day, at our staff meeting, I got a tremendous round of applause from the psych staff. The whole hospital knew about it.

There were many interesting and valuable ideas that I learned that year. Still, it was in the context of a one-on-one relationship with the patients. It allowed me to explore one person's life story and deeper emotions. The downside was that it limited my understanding of how that person built a healthy sense of self and dealt with challenges in their life every day. Going beyond those limits would be at the core of my practice.

BURNING AND ITCHING
DOWN BELOW

Each resident was in the outpatient psychiatric clinic in the second year. We had a caseload and supervision by the Director of the clinic. He was a rather forceful supervisor, and we had group supervision on a regular basis.

One patient I remember was a black minister with severe burning sensations in his genitals. His young daughter had a form of leukemia, and he had watched her put cream on her genitals. He could not resist looking. He could see her applying the ointment, and it greatly disturbed him. Eventually, his guilt was so severe that he developed the same symptoms as his daughter. Therapists would call this a "conversion reaction." It was rare, but it still required psychological help.

I worked with him for months, and the outcome was very successful. He was cured and gained several important insights about himself. It was gratifying because I learned a great deal while helping him. I was proud that I knew what to do at this stage of my training. I was learning I could think of myself as a psychiatrist in the same way that I learned to call myself a doctor. What I did mattered to both of us.

I did not learn much about treating the whole mind at the beginning of my training at the medical center. I learned a lot of theory but did not find it useful or helpful during the first two years of my residency. Years later, I realized that the time I spent learning and observing was in the back of my mind, helping me understand more about human behavior.

JIM MANN

One of the senior faculty was Jim Mann. He taught residents the skill of interviewing by having students watch him conduct an interview through a one-way glass. He came up to meet with us after to talk about what everyone had seen and what we learned. He was an excellent psychiatrist and a great teacher.

I did not know it then, but what I learned about interviewing would become critical to my work later. There was something else I took from my time with Jim that was as important as the interviewing skills and techniques I learned. When Jim interviewed people, there were no "softballs," a term journalists use for easy questions asked during the interview. Jim got to the heart of the matter and stayed there no matter how painful it was for the person being interviewed. I got in touch with a part of myself, determined to be as fearless as Jim.

THE BATES MOTEL

My entire residency up to this point had been very focused and limited to psychoanalysis. In my third year, I was in charge of a whole ward at Boston State Hospital in Mattapan, Massachusetts. I arrived at my assigned building at Boston State Hospital, and as I walked in, I was struck by the lack of any trees or flowering bushes outside.

Once inside, I was overwhelmed by the lack of bright colors or sunlight. The ward was filled with dark, depressing colors. A few chairs were scattered throughout the hallway, the bedrooms were sparsely furnished, and the one large meeting room was filled with a jumble of decrepit old institutional chairs. The physical appearance felt like the Bates Motel or some creepy place like Creedmoor Psychiatric Center. It was proof of what I'd read in a book called "The Mental Hospital " by Morrie Schwartz, who would later become a close friend. The book identified the destructive patterns of mental hospitals and had a profound influence on public policy.

I was a young doctor coming to a place filled with crazy people, and it felt *terrifying*. There was an expectation that I would know what to do for each of them since I was in charge of their care. I walked among people whose deepest thoughts and feelings were hidden and often unreachable. Most were psychotic, some were sociopathic, most were profoundly depressed or disturbed, and everybody was trapped in this place that was supposed to help them heal and get better.

I didn't know my role or how to work with such troubled people when I arrived. The patients tend to shuffle around or walk in a way that would be more fitting of the stereotypical mental patient from the movies. It reminded me of the film *One Flew Over the Cuckoo's Nest,* and I expected to see Jack Nicholson slowly walk down the hallway. The nurse's station was filled with medical and administrative trash. It was occupied by as many as 6 nurses and aides. I was supposed to be the Doctor who would help them get better. It meant getting to know them and what their problems were. More importantly, I needed to overcome my fear of them.

I came in not knowing anybody or anyone's circumstances. I had no experience with the hospital procedures or the 40 to 50 patients on my ward. That put me in an awkward position. It also exposed my deepest fears, prejudices, and attitudes toward the people and the environment in which they were captive. What does a resident in a training program like me do when the trainee is scared of the people they are supposed to be working with or, even harder, prejudiced against them as crazy, dangerous, and incurable? I was the Doctor, and the patients were my responsibility. One way or another, I must overcome my bias against the people I was there to cure. However, the cure for my bias would come in several unexpected ways.

It was only in the third year of my residency that I had an opportunity to learn some of the most crucial lessons I needed to be a psychiatrist. During my first two years, my training was very Freudian and psychoanalytic. I had a few patients and a supervisor, and we went into the deepest level we could on each patient to uncover their problems and issues. In the second year, I had more patients in the outpatient clinic. But we would still discuss the case, always one-on-one, never as a family or in a larger group.

In the third year, everything was different. I was assigned my ward of 40 to 50 people with mental health issues at Boston State Hospital. Many of the people in the group might have been there for months. I traditionally managed their treatment, with everyone sitting in a big circle meeting daily in the meeting room. It was a mixture of people from their 20s to their 70s. They would raise their hands to ask me a question, and Dr. Berens would give them an answer.

ASK THE HARD QUESTIONS

Dick Wolf, MD, was my senior supervisor during my third year of psychiatric residency. He was a straightforward psychiatrist and responded curtly to my questions, offering only enough to provide the answer to what I had asked. Yet his curt reply one day completely changed my outlook and approach as a psychiatrist.

My first serious case had me feeling everything I feared about the place. A young, totally psychotic 17-year-old girl was admitted. As I observed her, she appeared to be nervous and frightened. She was also hallucinating and withdrawn, like a small child wanting to hide in any space she could find inside herself.

My job was to help her come out of this psychosis, find out what was wrong, discover what happened to her, and why she was reacting so strongly. I went by the Freudian psychoanalytic book, conducted short and long interviews, and then asked her family to join us. They appeared very reserved, frightened, and nervous. I spent two hours interviewing them, asking the parents and the girl questions. I got no answers or insights into what caused her psychotic break. It felt like a complete waste of time. I was beginning to understand the complexity of psychiatry compared to medicine when you could remedy a problem with a shot or pill.

I didn't know the right questions because of my fear of

being thrust into a situation over which I had little control, coupled with my lack of experience. The ones I asked did not provide me with any clues or directions. I was afraid to push or probe because I unconsciously reflected her parents' fear of knowing the truth. It felt like I was skating on thin ice over quicksand.

I was smart enough to ask Dick Wolf to come in and help me. We set a time, and he joined me in the room with the patient and her family. Dick took charge of the session from the beginning. He wanted to know what was wrong, what happened, and how each person felt about the situation. Dick wanted to discover precipitating events and everyone's reaction to those events. His questions also focused on the family's positive and negative attitudes about things that happened in the family. I watched him as he relentlessly questioned the family and dug out the relevant family history and deeper issues and attitudes that formed a more complete picture. Dick effectively set the stage for the interview. Hence, the family knew he was in charge and would get to the bottom of every situation that had a bearing on this poor girl's state of mind. I became an attentive observer, watching and learning.

It turned out that the family was an extremely religious Catholic family. Her sexual relationship with her boyfriend made her feel incredibly guilty. The family was extremely judgmental and threatened her with burning in hell. The turning point was when we realized the girl genuinely believed she would go to hell because she was having "sinful sex" with her boyfriend. Her belief that she was going to hell was so powerful that a psychological break was her only escape. Dick spent no more than a half hour with them, and gradually, the girl became less and less psychotic until she was almost her normal self when she realized that what she had done would not consign her to fiery damnation.

By the time Dick finished, he had learned what was happening, put the pieces together, and figured out how they were all part of the problem. After the session was over, I asked Dick a simple question. "What did you do?" I had failed to get to the heart of the matter and help her the way Dick had. He told me something that changed how I thought about myself as a therapist. He taught me that you have to *ask* the hard questions and not back off from that role as the adult in the room. The family needs you to be the person who relentlessly pursues the crucial information. His lesson was to be fearless and ask the hard questions.

He reminded me that I need to be fearless. I knew starting when I decided to be a psychiatrist that being fearless was critically important. However, I was still somewhat hesitant and shy. Jim Mann reinforced that idea years later, and I was getting closer but was still not at the level Dick Wolf demonstrated. Now I was taking a Ph.D. level course in fearlessness taught by Dick Wolf, and I would never look back or be afraid to ask the hard questions ever again.

When I interviewed the girl, I was afraid to probe into areas I imagined would be too private. I never talked with her about the relationship with her boyfriend or explored her deeper guilt feelings. I hesitated to enter into that part of her life. When Dick said, "Don't be afraid to ask the hard questions," my heart jumped. Dick Wolf was not afraid to push and probe. He asked the hard questions. He was very supportive but only stopped once he had the whole story.

I realized that Dick went right to the heart of the matter and didn't flinch when people reacted strongly. He just kept going and going, pushing and probing. I finally learned I was the doctor and had to act the same way. I had to be fearless, relentless, and courageous. I had to help my patients understand aspects of their minds that they couldn't easily reach or understand on their own. It finally hit home and was a compelling lesson that transformed me as a therapist.

I realize there is no other way to conduct myself as a psychiatrist in every case. I could suddenly clearly define my role. I discovered who I needed to be regardless of how I felt about anybody or my inadequacies and fears. It was the most important lesson I could learn, and it stuck. I took the lesson to heart because the sense of being useless, not helping anyone, or having the tools to do what was needed was incredibly painful.

I felt ashamed of my lack of understanding of the obvious but excited to begin understanding what it meant to be a psychiatrist. It was powerful and liberating. I could imagine changing my approach, and it felt wonderful. I had no idea why it took all those years, from med school through my internship and this far into my residency, to learn this invaluable lesson.

The price you pay for excellence is based on the many, often challenging, lessons you need to learn. Dick Wolf taught me to ask the hard questions. That idea became the lighthouse in what was too often an uncharted and chaotic storm.

My sense of knowing the right thing to do changed everything. It was so uplifting that I was no longer defensive. I was happy; I wanted to get something meaningful done for these patients on my ward. For me, it was a newfound sense of freedom.

PATIENTS ARE PEOPLE FIRST

I would conduct a group meeting for the entire ward using the standard approach every day. They met with me daily for an hour to an hour and a half. The usual format was explained to me, and I assumed that was how things needed to be done. So, I proceeded every day in the same fashion with the same group of people.

It never occurred to me during these sessions that anyone else in the room was getting anything out of the discussion between me and the patient asking the question. I wondered whether anyone else was listening, interested, or found the information I gave to one patient valuable. I never asked anyone else in the group for a reaction to the question being asked. As far as I was concerned, they were sitting there, lost in their own world, feeling that the questions and answers had nothing to do with their life.

I did this same meeting every day. I know now that I was scared to know any deeper issues that each of them might have that I could not handle. My fear needed to be overcome. I needed to see the group as individuals, not lump them together and consider them my patients. I was coming to help each of them get better regardless of appearance. My fears colored the entire meeting and had to be changed. My fears were getting in the way of clearly seeing the people in the room.

One day, I was lucky enough to have a British Psychiatrist visit my ward. He was polite and extremely soft-spoken. I recall that he was also very tall, probably in his early 70s, relatively thin, and fit with a crop of neatly brushed-back white hair. He wore an impeccable three-piece blue pinstripe suit with gleaming black shoes. He came to study and observe and asked me if he could sit in on my group meeting. He ended up teaching me one of the most important lessons of my residency.

I ran the meetings as usual by having all my patients sit in a circle and raise their hands to ask me questions. On this occasion, he sat next to me during the meeting. After some time had passed, he leaned over and asked me if it was okay for him to say something. I told him absolutely. Some part of me knew there was a better way to conduct the group and help my patients.

He then turned to a woman on the opposite side of the room and asked her a simple question. "Do you know the woman sitting next to you?" Of course, she responded, "No." He told her, "Well, isn't that important since you're here in a psychiatric ward where you need to better understand what it's like to connect with people and develop friendships so that you're not so lonely and that your psychological state is improved." He implied that some social problems might be why they ended up here.

The moment he asked the question, even before the patient answered, I went into a trance state, which I can only describe as a dissociative reaction. I was not in the room for what seemed like a long time. My response and participation at that moment would look perfectly normal; however, in my mind, I suddenly found myself in a state of shock. It dawned on me that everything I had been doing with these patients was wrong. I saw that it was not just wrong but counterproductive. I was creating a hierarchy with how I acted out my role as the doctor. I needed to realize they were people first and patients second.

I was amazed. This unexpected moment changed my entire outlook. I used the Freudian psychoanalytic approach that had been the basis for my education. This was new, different, and better. The people in the group could learn about each other and understand each other. They could be a resource for one another, communicating with each other instead of having everything go through me. I felt I betrayed these patients. I didn't know that they could do their own work.

My experience was striking, regardless of what it looked like on the outside. I instantly recognized the shift in thinking this therapist from Britain was showing me. My new role was to help these people relate to each other as human beings, understand each other, and see and hear each other. My real purpose was to create a healing community of understanding, appreciation, and expression. The stark contrast between what I was almost mindlessly doing and what I suddenly realized I needed to do was triggered by the British therapist asking a simple and direct question. What he asked in just a few words had produced a complete shift in my thinking. It was as if the universe had gone from earth-centered to sun-centered. It was another major turning point.

I could not talk about my feelings until I met with him afterward for lunch. I understood that he did not think about the patients as weird or crazy but saw them as people. It was wonderful to realize that I would remedy my mistake and put the entire ward on the right track. My only regret is that it took three years to learn. I remember thanking him for showing me an approach that helped the people in the group and stopped me from feeling that I needed to always be at the center. The emotional transformation that took place inside of me was remarkable.

I said to myself, *"Wait a minute. I don't have to do this alone. I can get the patients to learn to reach out to each other. I don't have to have all the answers. I didn't have any of the answers. The people in the group would learn to express themselves, understand each other, and help each other. That new process would be part of their cure, and it was the right way to do it."* It was a new understanding of my job and how I might create a more meaningful role for my patients.

That moment with the British Psychotherapist was absolutely remarkable. Watching him in the group gave me a new awareness of how to do therapy correctly. During my third year, I took some courses in theater work as part of learning about Gestalt Therapy. This approach to therapy was very different from what I had been trained to do. I imagined all the possibilities of Gestalt and theater with this group of people I was working with. I knew we would have a very different experience. Going forward with a new way of running the group and doing therapy without precisely knowing what I needed to do provoked some anxiety and stress. But those feelings were minor compared to how confident I became.

Knowing and seeing the people in the group as individuals and not just patients made me feel as if the challenge to get to know everyone and help them could be too difficult. Being on a kind of Freudian autopilot, asking the right questions in the circle every week, and giving the same answers was much simpler and more manageable. I decided to try what I believed was the right thing to do. It was amazing how dramatically and quickly a profound transformation took place in the group and, more importantly, inside of me.

I started the new approach by asking the same question the British therapist had asked. I instituted a new way for every patient to participate. We broke into smaller groups with specific topics, discussion groups that discussed whatever was on people's minds, and a personal expression group that allowed individuals to explore their feelings more deeply. There was a dramatic change in those meetings, and they became exciting and fun, and most importantly, they were meaningful. Every patient had an opportunity to participate in a smaller group for discussion and raise important questions or to get help from other patients hearing about their life experiences. I was always aware that important and good things would happen when each patient learned how to relate and be known by one another.

It was these simple events, the ones that, on the surface, were so innocent, that became the most significant lessons for me as I evolved. Dick Wolf taught me to ask the right questions and be the fearless adult in the room. The British Psychiatrist asked one of the people in my therapy group if she knew the person beside her. All he did was ask a question as if the question itself was a lock that opened the minds of the people in the group and became a doorway to their souls.

I had the mistaken idea that lessons like these learning moments were supposed to be a painful realization that I was wasting time and had the wrong idea. Instead, I felt good that I was open enough to know what was happening at that moment. It cascaded from that small lesson to a whole paradigm shift, a complete shift in the meaning of what I was doing. My sense of myself and my growth and evolution as a psychiatrist and a person changed in those serendipitous moments.

THE SURPRISE PARTY

After six months, I had to leave my patients and continue my training. I walked onto the ward last morning and opened the doors to the group meeting. My surprise left me speechless. The room was decorated like it was someone's birthday party. I quickly realized it was a different party. All the patients had put together a display in honor of me and our time together. Food, confetti, multicolored balloons, and paintings were gifts for me. We spent the morning together, and I was incredibly moved.

I spoke with all of the patients, and they talked with each other. It was a celebration of our time together, filled with gratitude for the months we experienced together. When we spoke, they told me they were incredibly grateful for the changes I made after the "fellow from Britain" visited. I looked into their eyes and saw appreciation for what we had done since that morning. It was so moving and profound that I began to cry, and then everyone cried and hugged.

The contrast between my last and first days was impossible to ignore. I knew I had helped them, and they, in turn, transformed me. In the beginning, I was scared and unavailable. I entered a place filled with crazy people that reminded me of a horror film. I had been changed into someone who opened his heart and soul to people in need. I felt they had treated and cured me of something I had been living with and brought with me on my first day. It might have been my imagined fears, a sense of inadequacy, a lack of understanding of my purpose in life, or even my role as a psychiatrist. On that last day, I realized our work together had changed an entire group of people from strangers to friends and transformed me into a better therapist and, more importantly, into a better person.

I felt that I had gone from a dark and scary place to somewhere else that was bright and filled with light and love. From then on, I was in touch with the power of my commitment to truly understand the people who came into my care. It was a stroke of luck that the British Psychiatrist showed up and asked the question that gave me a new sense of myself, of my role as a therapist, and of, in some way, life itself. After that day, he just disappeared like a guardian angel, and I will forever be grateful to him and the people with whom I worked on that ward.

I was sad to say goodbye and leave Boston State Hospital in Mattapan, Massachusetts. I was not as excited as I had hoped by my next stop at the Air Force base in Grand Forks, North Dakota.

WEAPONS OF WAR - GRAND FORKS, NORTH DAKOTA

After I left my ward at Boston State Hospital in Mattapan, Massachusetts, I went to the Air Force base in Grand Forks, North Dakota. The USAF base is located in the northeastern corner of North Dakota, north of Emerado and 16 miles west of Grand Forks. At that time, we were in the thick of the Cold War. The base was a strategic site for B-52 bombers loaded with nuclear weapons always in the air and underground silos for Minuteman ICBMs. I was the only Psychiatrist on active duty. The culture was about duty and honor, and the code was always macho. I had to get used to so many men saluting me as an officer. I quickly learned to properly salute back.

After I married Avis, my first wife, I had to put in for 2 years of service. We bought a car and drove out to the base. We were set up with a lovely house, and I had an office for myself staffed by an airman who would greet patients and give them forms to fill out. I could make my own hours and determine any procedures I wanted to use. But I was expected to take my turn at on-call responsibility like anyone else.

My role at the Air Force hospital was easy since I was in charge of my department, made my own hours, and selected the patients I would see. I did have to take the same rotation as everyone. One Sunday, I was on call and ended up seeing ninety people. The other doctors congratulated me for working hard and handling all those problems without asking for help.

Not long after I arrived, I was on call with one of the interns, and we received a report that a General was in trouble. He came in with severe chest pains, and the intern examined him. The results were predictable, but the outcome was not. The intern told him to get to the hospital ASAP and start taking anticoagulants because he was having a heart attack. The general, who was more used to giving than receiving orders, told us he didn't need to go to the hospital; he would just run it off. I told him you don't run off a heart attack. You could die if you try. The intern said he could be treated so he would have a chance to live. The general did not listen, refused any treatment, and disappeared. We later learned he died on the track trying to outrun his heart attack.

I also had a unique role that no one else had. I became a civilian one day a week. I went into town to make myself available as a psychiatrist at the mental health center and the two-year medical school. So, on Wednesday, I wore my civilian clothes, drove into Grand Forks, and worked at the center, seeing patients and the school as a teacher.

I taught the interviewing techniques I learned from Jim Mann at Grand Forks to the medical students and nurses. One day a week, I went into town and taught at the medical school. It was set up at the Pentagon in collaboration with the state. I did live interviews at the medical school hospital that were beamed up to the class of medical and nursing students. After each interview, I came to the auditorium and took any questions the medical students or nurses had.

The Chairman thought I was courageous to lead the course

because there were two hundred students, each with different experiences and perspectives. They had many good questions, and we spent an hour discussing the reasons for anything I did in the interview. I had one memorable interview with a young man who came to see me because he was seriously depressed. I changed his prior diagnosis based on the new information I received during the interview. I canceled an elective ECT shock therapy treatment he was scheduled to get. It turned out he did not need the ECT, and when the class and I found out, I got a standing ovation from the students who had seen my interview. Working with the students and answering their questions made me think and learn more about interviewing. It was a gratifying experience that I thoroughly enjoyed.

Working on the base had many pleasant moments punctuated by challenging and disturbing events. Depression and anxiety seemed to be part of the job for the military stationed there. I tried to imagine what it would be like to always be on alert that you would be part of what could only be described as Armageddon for the entire world at any moment. It took its toll.

One serviceman who spent thirty years in the military with a family and 5 children committed suicide. He was in charge of men who loaded the atomic bombs onto the B52 Airplanes. He reported that his department was understaffed. The lack of adequate support posed a danger that could result in a nuclear accident. His requests to his commanders were ignored entirely. He felt betrayed by his superiors and his government. No one paid any attention. He was not my patient, but I heard about it, as did many other airmen.

It became even stranger when another airman at another North Dakota base, an airman with the same job and similar issues of feeling that he was betrayed because his superiors failed to listen to his concerns, also killed himself a few months later. A strategic base full of ICBMs and nuclear weapons being shuttled around on B-52s was an unbearable pressure cooker for even the strongest airmen.

Life off the base was decidedly different. The Director of the English Department at the university had the habit of pranking his staff once a year when they least expected it. Since I was a guest lecturer, talking to medical students about the process for intake interviews, he asked me to join him in one of his more elaborate pranks at the annual English Department dinner. He told his staff that I had been a basketball star when in college – obviously the Point Guard since I was not 6 feet tall – and I was going to give them a talk about the psychology of basketball according to Freud. I stood in front of his staff with a straight face, introduced myself as Dr. Berens Psychiatrist, and described the impact of oedipal anxiety on players taking foul shots. If a player's conflict with his oedipal unconscious were significant, it would impact his ability to 'put the ball in the hole.' It sounded great; for all I knew, it might have been true. The staff was deeply disappointed when we revealed it as part of an annual joke. After talking with them afterward, they all liked the Freudian interpretation of the foul shot. I wasn't sorry to disappoint them.

Doctor Jim Hoyne was the medical school's Chairman of the Psychiatry Department. During my two years there, we became good friends. He wanted me to stay in Grand Forks when my time in the service was up and become part of his teaching staff. I turned the offer down despite feeling it validated my work. The proposal added to my sense of self-worth, but North Dakota was just too far away from the places where I wanted to live and set up my practice.

NEWSWEEK WANTS TO KNOW

One day, while I was at work, I was contacted by a Newsweek reporter to get a story about Grand Forks. The magazine wanted its readers to know what life was like on a strategic air and missile base. There was nothing I was allowed to say. Everyone in charge of the base was paranoid about negative information being given to the press. They were extremely careful to cover up any problems or issues. The truth is that there were problems at Grand Forks that I wish I could have said to the reporter. Stories about the macho general trying to outrun his heart attack. The airman with 30 years in the service felt betrayed by his country and saw no alternative but to kill himself. Another airman in the same position at a different strategic base in North Dakota had the same response to the indifference of his superiors regarding the nuclear weapons under his control. He also could not face what might happen and killed himself. Newsweek never identified those problems, and I could not tell those stories. I did not take the risk that might have saved lives on the bases because I followed the rules that dictated silence.

AVIS

Before coming to my new assignment at the Air Force base in Grand Forks, North Dakota, I had been seeing Avis. It would be cold and lonely in North Dakota, and we decided to get married for reasons I no longer remember. Soon after the very elaborate wedding, we bought a car and drove to Grand Forks and the Air Force Base, where I was stationed as a Captain. We were given a lovely house and settled into the routine at the base. I had my own department.

Looking back from where I now sit, I realize I should have never married Avis. I did not feel the level of trust and love I had with Addie.

I believed she wanted to marry a Jewish doctor more than she wanted to get to know who I was as a person. When we were together, we just got along. It felt very depressing. Only the activity at the hospital allowed me to engage with the world and feel focused and alive. Once again, my professional life was successful and engaging. Yet, my personal life was a failure.

The time at the Air Force base passed, and we moved to Boston. We rented an apartment in Cambridge and then bought a house in Arlington. I had some friends who were psychologists, and we often would get together with them. Divorcing Avis was becoming the obvious conclusion. As a result, she slowly withdrew from our relationship. My practice and new friends were all I needed. After several months, she moved out to her own apartment. I stayed in the house and continued to grow my practice.

Once again, I was saved by my profession. My role as a competent doctor and a new practice as a therapist gave me a strong sense of myself. By contrast, my personal life was not. I was very down about my marriage to Avis and failed to understand myself as a whole person. I was there as Doctor Berens but absent as Howard, the Husband. The contrast was striking. There was no great pain or all-night conflict that I went through with Addie. I could say to Avis and myself that we should not be together and not feel guilty ending the relationship. The divorce went through without a hitch, and I was once again single.

I DREAM OF GHOSTS

It was reminiscent of the trauma I experienced as a child when my mother had a miscarriage, and I lost what would have become my only brother.

I was with my very pregnant mother in our living room when her water broke. Amniotic fluid and blood gushed out from under her dress onto the carpet. I was only four years old, scared beyond measure, and could do nothing to stop her miscarriage.

Until this point in my life, I had not spent much time thinking about my lost brother. I was an only child. One evening, after my divorce from Avis, I was alone in my house, relaxing on the couch before a warm fireplace. I was watching the shadows dance lightly on the ceiling.

I slowly drifted into a long dream about my dead brother. I imagined what it would have been like had he lived. It was so real, so vivid and profound. I loved having him in my life. In the few hours the dream lasted, I imagined him alive. I loved him. He and I were best friends. We did things together in my dream, and I watched over him as the older brother.

Suddenly, as I awoke, the dream began to fade, and my brother once again had to die. We said goodbye forever. When I awoke, I was crying and could barely stop. How sweet it was to bring him alive. I experienced a deep longing and a feeling of loneliness that was so deep it was beyond description.

I thought life often brings you pain, and you can do nothing about it. I wondered if I, on some unconscious level, was still grieving.

My mother was rushed to the hospital and almost died from eclampsia, a very preventable disorder brought on by high blood pressure that should have been monitored. I felt so angry at the negligence of the doctors who failed to prevent her illness. The anger and loneliness went on and on, and they felt like they would never stop. In many ways, I believe that was one of the reasons I chose to become a doctor.

LSD BY THE POND

I had finished my medical internship and established my practice as a psychiatrist, but I felt lost and depressed. Everything in my life was feeling empty. I spent my time feeling like I was not there, acting out the parts I was assigned to play. My heart was hurting from my practice and experience with the Air Force to my divorce from Avis. Despite all I had accomplished, I searched for joy and a new purpose. I only vaguely remember what it felt like before I was married and happily challenged by learning to be a doctor. I longed to have it back.

I rented an old farmhouse for several summer months in the rural western part of Massachusetts. It was an old two-story house surrounded by fields gone fallow and woods filled with old-growth oak. The house was isolated from everyone and everything. It was perfect for the absolute solitude I needed. In its way, it was a farm that had lost its purpose and feeling of joy. I was hoping being there would lead me to discover a new purpose and sense of joyful living.

One of my friends knew I was alone in the farmhouse, trying to become unstuck and move forward. He had weathered his crisis and wanted to help. He offered to take an LSD trip with me. At that point, LSD was an experimental and legal drug being explored by doctors and therapists worldwide. I felt out of touch with myself in so many ways and believed it might help guide me to a more conscious decision-making process and help me find a new purpose and sense of joy.

We talked about "the trip" for almost an hour, and we both took a pill containing LSD and gave it a chance to work. I was comfortable having another medical doctor on the premises. He said he would be there for me if anything went wrong. We were lying on the bare wooden farmhouse floor, listening to Mahler's Symphony Number 5. It was a fantastic experience listening to one of my favorite pieces of music.

After the incredible last notes echoed in my head, my friend decided to go outside to experience the forest. He left, and I started feeling scared and alone. His company had been more reassuring than I knew. So I stayed on the floor for a while and suddenly felt an overwhelming need to look outside at the small pond a few yards behind the old house.

The water was cold, clear, and empty, danced upon by the occasional Water Strider and other bugs living there. I felt a powerful need to stare at the surface. I sat cross-legged in the summer's weeds by the water's edge, thinking this strange thought. *Do I want to live my life under the water, or do I want to live my life above it? And what did that mean? Did it mean that my professional life would be exciting and fulfilling, but my personal life would be dull and repetitious by comparison?*

To live below the water, to live unconsciously, would be boring. It would mean having a standard everyday practice, doing the same prescribed therapy again and again, getting married and living in a hum-drum wealthy suburb, letting the years drift by until there was nothing left to drift. It would mean being alone and randomly walking through my professional growth. I would eventually stop growing and go through the motions until there were no more motions through which to go.

To live above the water, consciously and mindfully, meant I could challenge myself, explore and discover who I was, learn what was new and exciting, and constantly grow and improve professionally. It would define the rest of my life. I would look for mentors who could guide my growth and go where I needed to find new and better ways to be a psychiatrist. I would keep moving and changing, getting better until I was an old man.

I had the terrifying thought that my existence at that point was being determined for me. I felt like I was living below the water, slowly sinking more each day, unable to breathe, with no way to change it or determine how I wanted to live. I believed that most of my life was under the water, and the part I felt was being lived consciously was just an illusion. Looking at myself from some objective distance, as I had been trained to do, I could see that my life just happened day after day regardless of what I thought about who was in charge.

What would it mean to have control over my choices instead of being pushed and shoved by circumstances beyond my control? Was I brave enough to live a life above the water that would be extremely rewarding but also incredibly challenging? Can I learn from every experience that transforms me and moves me forward? Can I walk away from those situations that held me back and stopped me from the challenges and growth I wanted?

I was there for a very long time, just sitting and staring at the pond as if it were a water-filled crystal ball that would tell me what to do. I just stared and hoped the answer would suddenly rise from the depths and float upon the surface, like a photograph in a developer bath. Some part of my brain realized a profound meaning in that question that touched me deeply and emotionally.

The time I spent by the pond changed my life. I realized it was one of those transformative moments that became the metaphor I measured myself against. I realize now it was enough to ask the question. I remembered some lines I read from Rainer Maria Rilke's *Letter to a Young Poet*: *"And the point is to live everything. Live the questions now. Perhaps then, someday, far in the future, you will gradually, without even noticing it, live your way into the answer."*

Today, I am 85, many years away from the water's edge, yet I still imagine sitting and looking at the surface of that pond. I may never find the answer, but I know it's one question that always needs to be asked. To live above or below, consciously or unconsciously.

To live above or below, I constantly ask that question to this day. This question helped provide direction for the rest of my life.

WHAT GROWS IN THE GREENHOUSE

After completing my 2-years service in the Air Force, my final divorce from Avis, my profound experience at the pond, and the end of my marriage to Avis, I returned to my private practice back in Massachusetts, emotionally exhausted but with a renewed sense of purpose. Looking for new and better ways of helping my patients, I joined Greenhouse, a collective of fifteen therapists. We shared the rent on an old three-story house in Central Square, Cambridge, with several rooms available for therapists to use for psychotherapy. The group members were outstanding psychologists who believed in various new, but not necessarily psychoanalytical, approaches to therapy. They believed in exploring alternative ways of doing therapy. I was the only Psychiatrist in the group, and my training and knowledge added a level of depth and understanding that all of them listened to and valued.

We met regularly to share our experiences providing therapy. We would talk about each other's cases and discuss our therapeutic approach in what was always a respectful and supportive environment. I loved the collaboration that allowed me to compare the thinking and insights of people with very different training and backgrounds.

It began my lifelong journey of learning new and valuable ways of working with people. My formal training gave me an essential basic understanding and insight into the mind's workings. However, It was still too narrowly grounded in Freudian psychoanalytic concepts and approaches. Greenhouse was the start of having my mind, and heart opened to some new ways of doing therapy.

One year ago, Greenhouse decided to run a Carl Rogers workshop. Carl was one of the founders of humanistic psychology. He developed the person-centered, also known as client-centered, approach to psychotherapy that focused on unconditional positive regard for the patient instead of seeing them as a person who was mentally ill and needed a doctor to cure them.

We spent almost a year preparing the program. We rented a large conference space in Central Square in Cambridge for the 150 people who signed up to attend. It was my first experience helping to organize an important conference. I had a chance to learn from the person who developed what would become a cornerstone of therapy. I learned to recognize and trust people's potential to grow, heal, solve their problems, and meet overwhelming challenges.

During the conference, I learned to recognize and trust human potential by providing my clients with genuine empathy and an unconditional positive perception of who they are and could be. It redefined my role to be the person who was there to help facilitate change and offer support and guidance. My job was to provide a structure enabling clients to discover their solutions. It was, amongst other vital lessons, an education in self-awareness. I never hesitated to adopt what I learned from that workshop.

Person-centered therapy was at the forefront of the

humanistic psychology movement that I was beginning to understand. After the workshop was over, Carl gave me a big hug and thanked me for helping to organize the conference to be a success.

MORRIE

The most important person I met at Greenhouse was Morrie Schwartz, a full professor of Psychology at Brandeis. He wrote a book called "The Mental Hospital" that identified the destructive patterns of mental hospitals. That was my experience at Boston State Hospital in Mattapan, Massachusetts. The book had a profound influence on public policy. But as famous as he was, Morrie was humble. I have a long list of attributes for this amazing man that include kind, moral, fair and honest, trusting, and above all else, brilliant. He made quite an impression on me.

You could not ask for a better friend. At Greenhouse, Morrie introduced me to Vicky, my second wife. Morrie and his wife were often invited to our house in Newton for Thanksgiving and other holidays. I have intense feelings about him to this day. It was because he always shared his authentic self with me. He always respected people's opinions and ensured he acknowledged their points of view in every interchange. Everyone could feel his compassion and respect for others, which flowed effortlessly from his heart. Whenever I saw Morrie, I felt warmth and happiness. It's lovely to love someone and know they value that you care about them as much as they care about you.

As a full professor of Psychology at Brandeis, Morrie was endowed with the Chair for his work on his book showing how counterproductive the mental hospital environment was. He rang the alarm that mental hospital environments were hurting and not helping people with mental health conditions. Morrie's thoughts and ideas expressed in his book effectively changed the entire system for the better. Everyone admired and loved him, from the patients he saw in his clinical practice to his students attending his memorable lectures. Morrie died of ALS in 1995, much too soon and far too young.

The variety of relationships that happen in our lives is incredible. Some are wonderful and nurturing, and some are a source of terrible anxiety and pain. As a friend, he was the best one could hope for. Years after he's gone, I miss him and sometimes cry when I think about him. The lesson for all of us is to value and protect our relationships with good friends; they are rare and will not last forever.

VICKY

While I was at Greenhouse, my friendship and love for Morrie increased. I trusted him implicitly. One day, during a break in a workshop, Morrie was standing with a few people and introduced me to a very pretty lady named Vicky. I liked her right away, and I assumed it was mutual. We sat together and started talking and made plans to meet afterward. It was the start of a relationship that became marriage number two.

Vicky and I continued to date and enjoyed hiking, camping, boating, and being outdoors. We were developing a close and caring relationship and were having a good time together. Vicky lived with two other roommates and Shondra, her seven-year-old daughter from her previous marriage, in an apartment on the South Shore.

Part of my attraction to Vicky was that I saw her as self-reliant, a trait I looked for in all my serious relationships. Like Addie, she was not stuck constantly needing to be rescued like my mother. She was extremely confident when it came to dealing with any situation that occurred. Vicky worked as the Director of a small organization working with disabled people, writing grants, and running the day-to-day operations successfully.

After less than a year, we all lived together in a small apartment on Fayerweather Street in Cambridge. Vicky became pregnant, and we had our first child, a girl we named Jessie. We decided soon after Jessie came to get married. Vicky was pregnant again, and we decided to have a wedding on the Beach on Nantucket. It was a beautiful day; we were outside by the ocean, and we had written our vows, which were lovely and romantic. I had become a husband again and Shondra's stepfather. Vicky and I were one, for better or worse, in sickness and in health.

The apartment in Cambridge was already becoming crowded. With another baby on the way, I started looking for a new place to live. After several months, I bought a large house on Cabot Street in Newton, a few blocks from where Morrie lived. Everyone had their bedroom, and there was room for more.

The day we were getting ready to move to the Newton house, Vicky went into labor, and our son Dylan was born. I had a strong feeling of closeness from our two babies' birth, which has become even stronger as I grow older. I will write more about my love for them later since these feelings are very important to me, and I have held them close to my heart my whole life. It always feels nice to love someone you know appreciates it, and I knew my kids did.

After many years passed, our marriage started unraveling as the kids grew, and Vicky and I became more distant, that feeling of closeness that I prized gradually disappearing. In addition to her full-time job as a school psychologist, Vicky got her Doctorate with high marks. She had a small private practice in one of the rooms in our house. There was a fireplace and sliding doors, a waiting area, and parking for her clients. It was all very suitable for her small practice. One day, something happened that ultimately would change everything.

I was playing with Jessie, and she accidentally scratched me in the left eye. It was severe enough that we went to the Mount

Auburn ER, where I was given a shot of morphine and an eye patch. I quickly realized the doctor had given me too much morphine, and I passed out when I went home. I awoke with terrible chest pains and difficulty breathing that turned into a chest infection that lasted three weeks. It was severe enough that I passed out twice and gasped for air all evening for several weeks. I needed to put my practice as a therapist on hold while I was sick. I had no idea if it was acute and temporary or could evolve into something more chronic and long-term.

Because of the uncertainty of the outcome of my illness, Vicky expressed her concern about my ability to take care of the family. She believed I no longer wanted to work. She hit a nerve that started a cascade of deep-seated, uncontrollable feelings from my past. I became furious, filled with a rage that was surprising and sudden. Instead of realizing what I was experiencing, I completely withdrew. I imagined I was being accused of turning into my horrible, lazy father, a man who proved incapable of taking care of his family. It also touched another raw nerve I had been harboring. There was a growing suspicion that Vicky only loved me when I was healthy and working, not when I was sick.

The truth is that I was getting older. I always thought I would have unconditional love that would last until death do us part. I took great care of myself, but illness was always in front of me. My best friend Morrie had been diagnosed with incurable ALS and was going downhill fast. I became obsessed with the idea that if she could not handle this level of sickness, what would happen if I became severely ill or bedridden? Would she take the kids and leave me? All of these thoughts and feelings collided, making me angrier. That anger grew until it was all I could feel. My expectation of unconditional love would have to wait.

We attended couples therapy for several months to determine what was happening. Unfortunately, the counseling did not help. Couples therapy has only one of two outcomes. For me, it was a clear signal that our marriage was over. I finally decided I could no longer stay in the relationship.

We all met in the playroom on the second floor, where they heard me announce I planned to leave. There was a mood of sadness in the room, and I felt afraid for the kids who would become the children of divorced parents. There were tears on everyone's faces. I was overwhelmed by the pain and loss I was causing, but I tried to be strong. I wanted to give Jessie and Dylan some sense that they would be okay. I only hoped that it would make them aware that even though their lives would be profoundly changed, I would always continue to love them.

Looking back at this part of my life, I am deeply grateful to Vicky for bringing our kids into this world. It was Vicky who gave birth to Jessie and Dylan. I cannot imagine my life without them. Despite my best efforts, my feelings toward their mother would often spill over, and my kids felt they had to take sides. I will forever regret using them to support my anger. I hope these words will help them understand what happened and why.

Giving someone a second chance is a way of life in this country, and I had my turn after my divorce. I was feeling lonely and depressed again. You do not need to be a psychiatrist to know it's not a great time to make decisions. I became briefly involved with an ex-patient. I sent a letter to the Psychiatric Board of Supervisors explaining what I was doing. I was surprised that it resulted in a reprimand for making such a wrong decision. It could have been much worse. I got a second chance. I'm writing about this so that you can hopefully stop yourself from making any critical decisions when you're in crisis and feeling terrible about yourself.

ON BECOMING A FATHER

This section of my life was initially titled "Being a Father." After reading it and thinking about the words, I changed it to "On Becoming a Father" because I realized something important. Parenting is a process that starts at my children's birth and continues until I die. In a sense, I am never a parent; I am always parenting, involved with the many changes and stages of the process.

I was forty-four years old when Jessie was born. Before my children arrived, it seemed that having kids was a burden. Now that I am older and have two kids, I realize what a blessing it is. My feelings for them are overwhelmingly warm and loving. I cannot imagine my life without them. I can't think of them as separate individuals. They are my kids, my flesh and blood, and I care about them more than these words can convey.

We had many enjoyable times before the relationship changed. There were lots of hikes, boating, and playing in the backyard we called 'The Circus.' I was always cheering for them. Dylan played many sports, especially baseball, and Jessie played soccer and other sports from when she was young until High School. I was always there cheering them on. They were, in many ways, my home team. Remember traveling around with her as a teenager, looking at colleges. I made a point to let her decide. She chose North Carolina State after feeling at home on the campus, even though my overprotective self wanted her to go to a school closer to Boston.

I always felt I was given a second chance as an only child to be a kid again in a family of kids. I believe they felt safe and secure. They knew they were good people with solid values. When I talk to them now, they sound like mature adults and behave in ways that prove they have a reliable moral compass. They can empathize with others, indicating they grew up healthy. They are my two best friends. As they were growing up, I tried to protect them as much as possible from feeling the tension growing between Vicky and me before the divorce.

My strong reaction of fear and concern can be traced to my childhood trauma of my mother's miscarriage and near death when I witnessed her miscarriage. I was a frightened little boy who was helpless, unable to do anything to improve it. It is perhaps the driving reason I became a doctor.

I was trying to find a role that would make me feel omnipotent. That way, I could save my kids whenever they struggled or had problems. This feeling took me into their lives as their loving father who was able to rescue them from any threat. It was the same fantasy I had as a child, being the savior to my mother. Feeling omnipotent was a way for me to deal with feeling helpless.

My kid's work and security is another area I worry about. As I often do, I can trace back to the total lack of security provided by my father and the hard times we lived through. Jessie is doing well financially, which is reassuring for me. She has her own very successful set of videography companies. Dylan is beginning to work for a U.S.-based company where he can still use his remarkable skills, talents, and education to continue his work. Still, my deepest feelings about their security are very troubling to me. I often experience a lot of anxiety about both, even though there is little basis for concern. It is a strong and persistent feeling that results from what I experienced in my family. I've learned from Dylan to express my irrational fears, prepare for the worst, stop fretting, and move on with my life.

Well into old age with children who are adults, we all need to be able to learn to let go. I can do that if they're okay. It's not easy if they're in trouble, upset, struggling, or missing something.

All of us face challenges and make mistakes. That is simply part of learning and growing. I need to learn to live with that feeling of helplessness when they are sorting out their adult lives and stop trying to be omnipotent. If they ask, I can give them my advice or wisdom. It's waiting to be asked, but I still find it upsetting.

Looking back on it now, I see that I was a "helicopter parent." In my case, it meant being a father who is always hovering, ready to rescue them or put a Band-Aid on a scraped knee at any and every moment. I must learn when to leave them alone, listen, breathe, be invited to help, and never think I can pull rank and tell them what to do just because I'm the parent.

The hardest lesson is that trying to help can be counterproductive. I can now begin to understand that my anxiety and worry are harmful. My kids often help me learn this to be a better parent. They have become the best teachers. I am slowly and surely hearing them and taking their lessons to heart.

Dylan and Jessie have been great teachers on this subject. Dylan especially has helped me understand that he needs me to accept his boundaries and needs as an adult. Listening and hearing what they say and accepting them as teachers has dramatically accelerated my learning to become a better parent.

My death means I will leave them to fend for themselves without me. After I die, I won't know how they are feeling or what they are doing. They could be in trouble and suffering; once I'm gone, it's impossible for me to know about it. It's very upsetting to imagine not being there for them in the role I always had when they were growing up. It has me needing them to be as happy and secure on their own as possible. I will not be here, but I know they will feel my love, respect, and pride for them, which can be carried on as they go forward in their lives.

JESSIE

After less than a year of dating Vicky, we lived in a small apartment on Fayerweather Street in Cambridge with her daughter Shondra. Vicky became pregnant, and we had our first child, a girl we named Jessie. She started life in a crib; a sunny bay window off the apartment living room was her first home. Jessie moved me from thinking that children are a burden to understanding the feeling of joy and profound love that a child brings with her birth.

Jessie is forty-one years old now, no longer a child who needs to be watched over and taken care of. I no longer need to be her daddy, always watching out for his little girl. It's taken me a lifetime to adjust. Still, I have finally assumed the role of parent to adult children. I have outgrown feeling overbearing, constantly needing to watch over them.

I have always been a very caring and loving father to Jessie. Despite whatever stress or hardships I have gone through, I have always found out how Jessie was doing. She tells me that the one thing she appreciates the most is that I always want to know everything going on in her life. It doesn't matter how long it takes; I love hearing her voice and finding out what Jessie is doing and feeling. She often reminds me that I was a supportive parent and never made her feel bad for having her own opinions or ideas. I always encouraged her to stand up for what's right and fair and support and accept people from all walks of life.

She may need to vent and share her goals for her house or business or talk about something else. I know it's important to be there for her. We have this game we play. I'll offer to pay for something she can't afford, and Jessie will turn me down. I'll offer again, and she will turn me down repeatedly until I usually win. It's my nature to be generous with my kids, even when they want to be independent. I know she is glad I am in her life, which makes me very happy.

I no longer worry about Jessie's safety and security. She has built on her own a wonderfully successful videography business. When she was young, I gave her a present she wanted: a video camera to make movies. She enjoyed it so much that I bought her a few more cameras and supported her pursuit of her hobbies of photography and videography. It's difficult for me or any parent to guess the impact what we say and do will have on children as they grow up. That camera was a seed that helped her become interested in filmmaking, leading to her career as an outstanding videographer.

As an adult today, she manages her own successful business and is happily married to a loving, caring man. They have many friends with whom they spend time in South Carolina. She is happily doing exactly what she wants to do.

Every parent has a past, and it's important to separate those ghosts from the living when it comes to your children. Jessie is an adult, and it is incumbent upon me to remember that and act accordingly. I must remember to keep my past fears to myself instead of projecting them onto her. I need to graduate from being a helicopter parent -- a parent who takes an overprotective or excessive interest in the life of their children and fights their battles and cannot let them fail – to being the adult parent to an adult woman who will be okay navigating the bumps in the road we all experience.

The divorce from Vicky was painful for me. Sometimes, that pain would seep out, and Jessie would hear the hurt and anger I felt. I would unwittingly put her in the middle, reacting to her differently than I did to Dylan. The daughter is usually closer to her mother. It was a rare occasion, but still, she would listen to my complaints and get upset. We have talked about it since it's critical to externalize the feelings she might have to not blame herself for anything I was saying. I know this is my issue and mine alone and that I was still feeling resentment about my divorce from her mother when Jessie was growing up. I look back on those leaks as I call them and feel they were moments of weakness, for which I am forever sorry they happened.

DYLAN

We were still living in the Fayerweather apartment in Cambridge and had just closed on the house in Newton. Vicky was ready to deliver the night we moved to the new house. She was packing right to the last minute until we went to Mount Auburn Hospital to deliver Dylan. After he was born, we took him home the next day to a house that was not ready for a new baby. His first few days and nights were spent in a big, carefully lined cardboard box.

Like Jessie, Dylan started his life in a secure and solid relationship. He grew up as an adolescent and young man in a family that was undergoing a divorce. Despite that, I know that Dylan has become a solid adult with a strong sense of himself and a good core of values. I remember that we had a lot of fun together. I had finished the basement of the house in Newton, and we spent many happy hours there playing ping pong and shooting eight ball or straight pool.

We fastened a basket to one of the columns in the basement for basketball, slightly higher than we were tall. We practiced our slam dunks, passing, and shooting techniques. I often attended many of Dylan's baseball games and coached the team for one year. Dylan was always a good athlete. I remember during the playoffs when he was in the 5th grade, suggesting that he change his batting style from a hit-it-into-the-bleachers swing to a more relaxed just-punch-it and not try to always hit a home run. I can proudly say that It worked. He had several good at-bats and even won an award from his coach for his hitting ability.

I always felt I was given a second chance as an only child to be a kid again in a family of kids. Dylan often told me that he was happy with the attention I gave him. When we were in the backyard in Newton, I'd hit the ball to him and call out imaginary plays and scores. When I hit a high-arching ball, Dylan acted like it was the top of the ninth inning and he was up against the imaginary outfield fence. We imagine that Dylan would grab what could have been a home run. Shades of me as a skinny kid chasing a pink stickball on a busy Brooklyn avenue.

All of us spent hours building a terrific train set and surrounding village. They both had many friends and happy birthday celebrations. And we spent endless hours playing with Sam, our golden retriever, in the house and backyard.

Despite my hurt and pain, I tried to compartmentalize what I felt as the divorce proceeded and not have those negative feelings spill over. It was always a challenge, yet I was always careful to try and do my best not to discuss the problems between Vicky and me or to say anything negative about their mother. Not being perfect, I sometimes fail, and all I can say now is I'm sorry if it caused him any pain in the past.

It's taken time, but today, my relationship with Dylan is better than ever. We have gone through many phases, some contentious and challenging for us. I ascribe it to the growing up process and separation that a son and father typically experience. Sometimes, even a loving father can try and run away when it becomes too painful to be in touch. But we made sure our differences healed, and we were better for it having happened.

As adults, we switched roles; he became the teacher, and I was the student. He is concerned about my health and has taken on the new role of teacher, encouraging me to be healthier. He has also helped me stop being a helicopter parent. He is helping me as I struggle to break the habit of projecting my anxiety and fears onto him. He is usually a patient teacher, and I need to learn many lessons he provides to be a better parent and healthier person.

There are moments when helping is not helicoptering. At one crucial turning point in Dylan's life, I directed him away from a crisis consuming him. I suggested he go back to school and get a Master's Degree. He has said that it was some of the best advice he has ever received and changed the trajectory of his entire life,

There is great wisdom in realizing that if your child is angry or upset with you, it's vital to hear them out and not pull rank and assume the role of parent. Being the adult in the room with your kids is an important lesson I've learned as a therapist. They – including Jessie – need to be on the same level as I am, one adult to another, not forever trapped in the parent-child hierarchy of my Brooklyn family. I've learned that even trying to help, again helicoptering into their life, can be counterproductive. My anxiety about Dylan only makes whatever he is going through worse. Once again, it is the past forcing its way into the present. It is about the connection between my childhood trauma, feeling helpless as I watched my mother almost die from her miscarriage, and my need to make sure Dylan is safe and secure.

What I need to realize is that he is a very smart and capable man. He has a graduate degree in sustainable agriculture, speaks fluent Spanish, and has an extensive and impressive resume filled with high-level work experience throughout

Latin America, a place he calls his "happy place" for international sustainable agriculture.

At certain times, it has been more challenging and, at other times, easier for both of us, separating the child from the father, Dylan, the son, from Dylan, the man. It is a process that has taken many years of work on my part, learning not to be overly helpful or involved with his decisions, struggles, and stresses. The antidote is to focus on his successes, strengths, skills, and self-awareness about his challenging choices and situations. It is so important to recognize his ability to take care of himself wherever he is working and living,

BOSTON FAMILY INSTITUTE

Several years after my divorce from Vicky, when Jessie and Dylan started thinking about college, I could again focus on my practice. Boston Family Institute was founded and operated by Dr. Frederick Duhl,

a psychiatrist. He worked with his wife, Bunny S. Duhl, Ph.D., a very competent experiential family therapist. It reminded me of Dick Wolf's dictum that you need to ask the hard questions. The Institute was an eye-opening experience into many new therapeutic techniques taught by Fred and Bunny and others who were excellent teachers.

My next step was to move beyond the strictly Freudian approach to psychotherapy I learned during my internship and residency. BFI was focused on families and marriages and believed in what they called the "inside out" approach. That meant that to fully understand the issues of a family or marriage, you needed to demonstrate the conflicts and problems inside the relationships. It was the reverse of being the doctor looking in from the outside.

I was introduced to many valuable approaches that I learned, including "family sculpting," a technique in family therapy that requires the family to try and arrange themselves in a way that portrays a significant, often troubling past event. This is done by asking one of the family members to be the "sculptor" and placing the other family members into a tableau that recreates the event scene. Changing the role of the sculptor was an exciting way to begin to see the different ways each family member perceived the event and gain insight into the family from the inside. I often wondered how this would have worked with the religious family I saw and the young woman who thought she was destined for hell.

Boston Family Institute was a place where I learned to integrate a tremendous amount of new and exciting therapeutic approaches. I never stopped valuing my original training; I just added what I learned from them. As always, I did not hesitate to apply the best lessons and ideas wherever I found them throughout my career. It was a perfect example of the value of being a lifelong learner and being open to new and exciting ways of working with people. Once again, I was going beyond the limits of my initial training as a psychiatrist to be the best therapist for my patients.

CALIFORNIA OR BUST

To keep changing, growing, and learning new ways of being a psychiatrist, I knew I would have to go and find other essential models. At this point in my life, Jessie and Dylan were in college, and I was no longer tied to Massachusetts. That led me to San Diego, California, and a month-long workshop in Gestalt Therapy with psychologists Erving and Miriam Polster.

There were about 20 people of different ages and backgrounds in the workshop. It was split between psychologists with their own practices and those working in a hospital. We met from morning till late afternoon Monday through Friday. Each person was expected to take risks and be open and authentic all the time. Erving was the workshop leader and worked with one person at a time as the rest of the workshop watched. When we felt that we were not our authentic selves, Erving would have us role-play as someone we felt was significant in our family or friends. For me and the rest of the group, it was often very moving and pertinent in each person's life.

When it was my turn to tell my story, I focused on my mother's miscarriage and the death of a brother I never knew. The memory had me crying. Even though it was not easy to completely open up in front of strangers, it was also very liberating. As Erving led me through the session, he showed me how powerful this approach could be. Once again, I was learning outside the narrow box of my formal training. During the workshop, I decided to incorporate the best of what I learned into my approach to therapy.

The Gestalt approach I first learned in the workshop led by psychologists Erving and Miriam Polster has been a part of my work ever since. This approach to therapy enables people to tune into their inner selves, address the past, and focus on the here and now. Some of the techniques dramatically differ from what I used during my residency. For example, suppose a client is having issues with a particular person. In that case, I can use an empty chair, ask them to imagine whomever they need to talk with and say whatever they need to say in a safe and secure environment. I have also used role play in which the client acts like someone who may be causing them problems.

All of this work helps the client become centered or focused in the present and get in touch with the emotions that are crucial for them to deal with. I often wonder how these techniques would have worked with my patients during my residency in a clinical setting like Boston State Hospital, where I was responsible for an entire ward.

MOVING THE CHAIR

Before he died from cancer, Dan Brown was my partner in our Cambridge practice. He was also my good friend and mentor. As the chairman of the Psychology Department at Harvard University, Dan was a renowned world expert on hypnosis. He often did workshops, saw patients, and talked with me about whatever he was learning.

Dan was far more intelligent than me and maybe all other psychologists, which is one of the reasons he was a great teacher and mentor. He knew much more than most professionals, myself included, about every aspect of human development. Various universities and colleges always asked him to teach psychology, emphasizing hypnosis. I was lucky to be his colleague every day. Collaborating with him inspired me to learn more about challenging problems and not be intimidated by them.

Dan's cases often fascinated me, and I appreciated his sharing the findings. Dan was a genuinely brilliant psychologist who contributed so much in his lifetime. It was an essential part of the trusting and caring relationship we had. One case, in particular, stands out. Dan spent lots of time in San Francisco interviewing Sirhan Sirhan. Under hypnosis, Dan discovered that a cult recruited Sirhan, utilizing hypnotic techniques to indoctrinate their members. According to Dan's findings, Sirhan was a hypnotized decoy in the death of

Robert Kennedy's shooting. Dan would describe the details of his many hours of interviewing Sirhan in jail through a glass screen and how hard he worked to discover what happened. It was as fascinating as it was instructive.

My friendship with Dan coincided with the divorce and child custody hearings Vicky and I were having. We did not talk about my personal life very much. Listening to Dan discuss his cases was like a timeout from my problems that helped me gain a better perspective on my life. His friendship made me realize there were other important things to consider and discuss than Vicky's feelings towards me. The opposite was true for Dan and his wife. They were in a loving and supportive relationship that they never hesitated to discuss.

I was doing family therapy as a co-leader with Dan Brown in his office at Harvard. We worked with a family of four – father, mother, 17-year-old sister, and 15-year-old brother. We started with me observing and Dan leading a family meeting. After some 40 minutes, we took a break, and Dan told me he was not progressing or getting anywhere. I asked him if I could try something that might work.

Inspired by an idea, I moved the father's chair closer to the 17-year-old daughter. Two minutes later, they were both crying and hugging each other. When they calmed down, the entire family opened up and revealed the family dynamic, causing much anguish. The father admitted he no longer felt attracted to his wife. The wife told him she also did not feel sexually attractive anymore. Still, she wanted him to continue 'loving her.' It was a new beginning for them. After much talking and flowing tears, the session ended with hugs all around, and they left holding hands.

Everything changed after moving the father's chair closer to his daughter. That move interrupted an ongoing game in which the mother positioned herself between them and controlled their interactions. Without recognizing this, the mother unconsciously formed an alliance with her daughter to keep control of the interaction and ensure the daughter always sided with the mother. She used her loving daughter to communicate her pain to the father and set up the game as "us" against "him." This is not bad behavior. It is a common finding in many families and organizations. The original way they were seated – mother between father and daughter - mirrored the family dynamic the mother was trying to establish. Therapists call this 'triangulation.' Moving the chair took away the mother's control and priorities, and the father and daughter could talk and share their feelings 'directly.'

Dan was extremely impressed by what I did that resulted in the changes in the family's dynamic and the insights it provided. He thanked me and told me that without my intervention, he would have been unable to get anywhere with the therapy he wanted to provide. I still smile today when I think about his praise for my simple creative idea. His respect for me increased my self-worth and made me feel I had a real role as a psychiatrist. It gave me a greater understanding of myself as a creative person willing to push my limitations to try and discover what I could find in myself that I could use in my work with my patients.

PSYCHOSYNTHESIS

The drive to be a continuous learner continued throughout my life. After working with Dan Brown, I learned about a new approach called psychosynthesis, which was another significant turning point in my life. Psychosynthesis was emerging at that time as a relatively new approach to therapy on the West Coast that was gaining popularity. I spent more than two years traveling to California from Cambridge, attending seminars, workshops, and counseling, appreciating the learning I gained from an exciting new therapy approach. I had the opportunity to work with some brilliant and experienced people developing and using this form of therapy. It was very different from the psychoanalytic approach that traditional East Coast therapists used.

My formal training was geared towards Freud and psychoanalysis. The goal was always to uncover elements of our adult mind tied to childhood experiences. At the time, years ago, Roberto Assagioli was developing a different approach he called psychosynthesis. His approach was a break with Freud. He believed that if there is an analysis of the human psyche, there also must be a synthesis that includes all the other parts of a person's life. Psychosynthesis was important for the therapy work I was doing and also for learning about myself.

The work I did in my studies of psychosynthesis helped me understand why I acted in certain ways that were limiting my growth. It made me think back to the pond and realize that my actions forced me to live below the water. My time in California helped me understand how psychosynthesis can be used to better empathize with my patients. It's a complex and fascinating subject that would take an entire book to adequately cover. I can only write about how I used and experienced psychosynthesis in my practice.

LOVE AND MONEY

I met John Ambrecht when he was taking a course in Boston. John was a well-known and respected attorney in Santa Barbara, California. His practice included helping families understand and consider the legal issues of inheritance and succession planning between generations. As we talked over dinner, he told me many of his cases were relatively straightforward. There were also the ones that seemed intractable and ended up going nowhere because of the emotional baggage and issues that John could not resolve.

I learned that every year, countless families pass their businesses, investments, real estate, and other assets from one generation to the next. This transition can be among their most complicated tasks, mainly when family issues arise. I had an idea that would help. We could form a consulting group that included John for the legal aspects, and I would help with the psychological issues. This was a fascinating opportunity to use my skills with people going through emotional upheaval when they needed to pass their significant assets from one generation to the next. I knew conflicts around these issues have emotional costs. They can create a more significant threat to the assets than taxes or financial risks. John and I set up a program that took an approach to both sides of the transition that we called *Families and Wealth*.

Our first client was a wealthy family agribusiness that was

referred to John. Farming in California is a multi-billion dollar business, with California as the fifth largest food supplier in the world. This family farm was one of the largest in the state. The company ran smoothly until one of the older and most influential members had a heart attack. The family needed to find how to begin to include the next generation to ensure the future of the business. John and I met with the adults who ran the company and their kids and devised a solid succession plan. We hired a 'monitor' to be embedded in the business after we left to help them stay on track. I knew that bringing the generations together and addressing key issues would open up many unexpressed feelings that had never been dealt with before.

An example of hidden feelings that surfaced happened when I worked with one of the children. He often comes to work late and leaves early. His father, a man who was a dedicated founder of the business, always came in first and left last during the week and even on weekends. The monitor reported the hours this son worked to the father, who initially directed his anger at the monitor for 'reporting' on his son.

As soon as I heard about it, I flew to California, knowing I needed to sit down with the father and son and talk. The father's anger and fears abated when he finally sat with me and his son. As I worked with them,

the son revealed that he wanted to be a real dad to his children. He wanted to be with his kids in the morning or attend soccer matches after school. He felt his dad was absent because he focused on the business. The father understood the message. He realized that his son needed a more balanced work-life that the father never had to successfully take over the company. It was a generational rift that no one expected yet required to be dealt with as part of the succession planning. It was also an example of the unspoken psychological pain and stresses that a family can experience when succession is being planned.

It became apparent to me that while the older founders had urgent concerns to make their business a success and bring security to their families, the next generation, having felt more secure, could feel the need to spend more time and devote more energy to their role as parents. It was very powerful and touching to watch the gap close between the generation of father and son. It was a lesson for them and an important lesson for me about the assumptions held by different generations and their perspectives on life that are usually never articulated or shared.

We invited a writer we knew, Tom Gorman, to develop a book called *For Love & Money* based on our consulting experiences. The book presents an approach to recognizing family dynamics as part of the succession process. I am proud to have developed the consulting group *Families and Wealth* and helped write the book *"For Love & Money."*

GOOD BRAKES

After a few years running my practice as a therapist in Cambridge, I spent two years as part of a Fellowship at Boston University Medical Center in Child Psychiatry sponsored by Boston University School of Medicine Medical Center. Those two years were a significant learning experience for me as a therapist and, even though I did not know it then, as a father-to-be. Our work with children gave me powerful insights into my thoughts and feelings. It demonstrated that I could be creative in my approach to therapy.

One example jumps to my mind. I was at the Cooper Community Center in Roxbury, Massachusetts. Jerry Steckler was my supervisor, and we worked with a group of hyperactive boys. One morning, we went outside to the playground. I watched one of the boys go up and down on the giant slide. I went over to him and recalled telling him, after he came to a hard stop at the bottom of the slide, that he had very 'good brakes.' I asked him to show me again how he did a great job stopping. He went back up and came down proudly, demonstrating his braking technique. I then asked him to go around and watch how the other boys used their brakes. He harnessed his hyperactivity and spent the rest of the morning watching and showing the other boys how to break their slides. It was a good approach. I was able to support his self-regulation skills and self-awareness.

I had previously consulted with the schools in Providence, Rhode Island, where I learned firsthand about child psychology. I was called to a classroom to see about a nine-year-old girl the teacher described as bizarre. As I walked in, the girl stood on a box, holding the teacher. When I walked over, the girl jumped onto me after the teacher introduced me as Dr. Berens. I remember telling her that leaping on me was an interesting way to say hello. I asked her if she could do it again, but not as hard. After she did, I said we should go around the class and see how other kids say hello. The teacher was delighted and later told me that the girl learned something important.

Again, it was an instinct I used, and it worked. I may have understood less than I would have liked about child development, but I understood the best approach. I started to trust my instincts, something that came to me quickly, becoming a lifelong habit.

THE DANGER OF NUKES

At the same time I was traveling to the West Coast and back, learning about psychosynthesis, I joined Physicians for Social Responsibility, a group of doctors and scientists concerned about the dangers inherent in nuclear power. We did workshops and appeared on local TV, trying to educate people on the tremendous hazards of atomic energy and, more importantly, the potential for global destruction resulting from using nuclear weapons. This had been on my mind since I spent time at the Air Force Base in Grand Forks, North Dakota, surrounded by world-ending ballistic missiles.

In April of 1986, an explosion at the Chornobyl atomic power plant resulted in one of the most severe nuclear accidents in history. The level of contamination with cesium-137 was the highest and most deadly ever recorded. Several members of the Russian Parliament came to meet with us at the Physicians For Social Responsibility headquarters in Cambridge. The delegation was worried that another Chornobyl was sitting somewhere in Russia. I attended several meetings with the Russians and members of the Union of Concerned Scientists (UCS), to which I also belonged. We recommended ways to mitigate the human toll Chornobyl was taking and suggested ways to stop another disaster from happening.

It was an opportunity to apply what I had learned to a more significant social problem, something I have been invested in doing my entire life. What I know about the human mind in an individual, one-on-one, or group setting can also be valuable when treating society's problems and issues.

I felt a strong sense of purpose in being active in this organization and have always held them in the highest regard. I was also very moved by our devotion to keeping an eye on the dangers society needed to avoid. We have to understand the risks here. It was good to be with others who shared the same feelings and efforts to address these critical problems.

I am a psychiatrist, and I am also a doctor. As a doctor, I am well-versed in nuclear contamination's medical and health effects and sinister impacts. As someone in any profession, one can often join industry groups or associations to conduct advocacy and have a stronger voice on issues. I recommend others follow their values because they can find a greater sense of meaning. Consider the various ways your profession crosses over into society and what you can do as a professional to improve things.

THE ASSASSINATIONS

While consulting with the school system, I met Bill Pepper in Providence, Rhode Island. Bill was starting an innovative program where he took high school dropouts and put them in a community house. He had a young couple supervising them. I remember he told me the couple was fantastic, musicians in their early 20s who the kids could identify with. They had a three-story house with the kids living on the top level and the couple on the first floor. Living in a home would provide inspiration to learn and grow instead of being unwillingly stuck in the school system where they were failing. I liked the plan and felt his ideas, and mine were compatible.

Bill asked me if I was interested in picking up on his other area of interest, the assassination of Martin Luther King. He wanted to determine beyond any doubt he had that James Earl Ray was the actual assassin. He said he could use my help to visit Memphis to interview James Earl Ray to determine if he was the shooter. I agreed and went there with Ralph Abernathy and attorney Mark Lane. This opportunity seemed worthwhile even though I had no idea what my role would be.

We stayed overnight in Memphis, and I remember FBI agents camped in a nearby motel. Bill wanted some psychiatric insights into James Earl Ray to help ascertain whether he could shoot Martin Luther King. Bill was always stretching his conception of what my role could be. I couldn't give him concrete advice about getting inside Ray's psyche. I felt slightly uncomfortable because Bill believed I could figure out something only a psychiatrist could understand. Still, I felt a strong sense of being involved with something important, which was enough for me.

I found myself working with Abernathy and Lane, all well-known people, trying to figure out who shot the bullet that killed King. I contributed ideas about what drove the social unrest and resulting assassinations. It felt like I was part of history instead of just a spectator.

I never gained much clarity as to what role I could play whenever we met, but Bill wanted me to be part of the team. It was a real opportunity to get an education behind the scenes in what had become a very crazy world. More importantly, it awakened something in me since I worked with influential people impacting my society and the world. I wanted to get more involved in politics and social change.

THE PSYCHOLOGY
OF POLITICS

My time with Bill and his team and my awakening to my newly added role as a social activist led me to my next project. After nearly a year of intense preparation, in May of 1991, I chaired the Harvard conference entitled "*Psychology in Politics.*" The meeting was held at The Center for Psychological Studies in the Nuclear Age at Harvard and co-sponsored by Boston University's McCormack Institute of Public Affairs.

I had been very disturbed by the political events that were going on in this country, especially how the public was being subjected to sophisticated psychological messages that attempted to push them to vote for the candidate paying for the message. It was pure and straightforward marketing designed to manipulate people's choices about politicians running for office.

The conference was a one-day working meeting attended by thirty politicians, mass communication experts, and psychologists. I created the conference by contacting every participant, explaining what we were doing and why it was necessary, and asking them to attend. It was both a joy and a surprise that the people who attended were all very knowledgeable and, in some cases, even famous contributors in their fields.

The day before the meeting, I had lunch with George Gerbner, the Dean of the Annenberg School for Communication. We had a delightful time, and he said that although he had published nearly three hundred articles, they all sat on a shelf. This meeting would allow him to meet face-to-face with people actively working in this field and discover connections and collaborations in real time that would not have happened otherwise. He was delighted to present at the conference, and his enthusiasm was very supportive. I knew that the other presenters would feel the same way.

The conference was a great success and provided value to many who attended. The attendees talked and listened to each other with interest and appreciation. I was prepared to develop more conferences, but as too often happens, the funding was not available at that time.

LAURA

When I was young, I often heard the expression, "People plan, and the gods laugh." I was never sure what that meant until I was caught in the undertow of the pond and, despite my most ardent desires, found that my choices were overtaken by circumstances forcing me to make a decision that left me feeling like a spectator in my life.

My son Dylan was going to school at the University of Arizona. I had become friends with a couple before they moved from Massachusetts to a small house outside of Tucson. Dylan decided to attend the University of Arizona. He found them to be good friends; in many ways, they also saw him as a good friend.

Late one spring, several years after my divorce from Vicky, I flew in from Massachusetts, taking time off from my growing psychiatric practice in Cambridge near the Charles River. We all met at Suzy's house every time I visited Dylan. Suzy's older sister Laura happened to be there. From the start, Laura made a tremendous impression on me. She was attractive, but more importantly, Laura was extraordinarily smart. She was a scientist with a Ph.D. in Biochemistry doing important research. After that first chance meeting, I often thought about her on the plane ride home.

I saw her again in the fall of that year. Her eldest daughter came to Cambridge to start her undergraduate program at Harvard and took a dorm room. Laura stayed at my 3-bedroom apartment near the campus in what ironically was Dylan's old room. I spent a week with them, going around Cambridge, looking at the shops and the Harvard Co-op, and checking out the great restaurants in Cambridge and Boston. We had a great time, and Laura and I spent many enjoyable hours discussing science and her research. She confided in me that she no longer wanted to be married and had decided to file for a divorce.

Later that night, we spoke about her feelings for me, and despite the short amount of time we had been together, I shared how I was beginning to feel about her. We were both so open and honest that being with her back then at that time in my life felt intimate and right.

Several months later, I went to Seattle to be with her again after Laura's divorce. She was attending a scientific conference focused on cancer research. We enjoyed going around the city, talking for hours in great restaurants, and spending romantic nights together. She was very affectionate towards me and was open about her life and feelings. The closeness and intimacy grew even stronger between us. I had met someone who could be a genuinely authentic and honest partner.

I did not have any doubts about us caring for each other. Laura was intelligent and deeply interested in science. Laura was emotionally open to who I was and wanted me to know her in a genuinely profound way. I felt safer and more relaxed than I ever imagined at that point in my life. It's hard to believe, but It happened again when I was older. But I'll get to that when I write about Karen.

Laura had taken a position as a staff professor at the University of California San Diego and moved from Arizona to California with her two girls. Her work was so exceptional that they provided Laura with her own lab. We both loved science and medicine, and our conversations were significant. She could teach me a great deal about subjects I deeply cared about. She published many good articles that I read and learned from as well. She had become a role model for me, not just a woman but an individual whose mind was intellectually exciting and challenging. She was someone who was contributing something important to the world.

I would travel to see her almost every other weekend, flying from Massachusetts to California. At one point, after a year of cross-country excursions, we got married even though it remained a long-distance relationship. I recall when I got off the plane and came down the ramp to see her smiling at me and welcoming me with such warmth and love. Leaving was becoming too complicated, and we needed to plan a way to be together. That was when the gods began to laugh.

After almost a year, Laura and I got stuck. The idea was that she moved somewhere on the East Coast or I moved west to California. Either one seemed impossible then and would create severe professional problems for each of us. She was an esteemed professor and researcher at the University of California in San Diego. I was a successful psychiatrist with a growing practice in Cambridge, Massachusetts. It was a terrible dilemma for us.

I wondered how I could take her kids that far away from their father, who lived and worked in California. How could I start a new practice somewhere new and make enough money for us to live on? Laura wanted to avoid taking her girls across the country away from their father or looking for another hard-to-find job as a professor and researcher with her lab. It was too much to ask from either of us, so we parted.

Our relationship didn't work out because of overwhelming circumstances. It was one of those times that I was pulled down to living below the water despite trying to live above and do what I felt was right.

LYNN

After Laura, my cross-country excursions that racked up frequent flyer miles stopped, and I settled into my practice in Cambridge, Massachusetts. I spent the next several years living alone, being single, and occasionally meeting new women on J-Date again. I was the type of man most women I dated would want to bring home to their mother - nice-looking, established, relatively wealthy, a Doctor. It was easy to meet my needs for companionship and intimacy. Several women might have become more than just a date, but I was still afraid of any real closeness or commitment. Until I met Lynn.

Lynn and I had several interesting online conversations. Then, we set up a dinner meeting at a restaurant on the East Side of Lower Manhattan. I came in from Boston and arrived early. I was waiting for her at the restaurant when she walked in. My first impression was that she was very attractive. Yet, another quality was much more interesting to me. She had this air as she walked in that seemed calm, self-assured, and at ease with herself.

We had a lovely time, and I was aware of her charm and maturity. After I drove her home to one of the Trump buildings on the Upper West Side, we made an appointment to meet next time at her apartment. When I went there on our next date, I saw her place beautifully furnished with tasteful furniture. We spent the evening sitting on the couch just talking.

It was lovely, and after that, we began feeling more intimate. I knew I was attracted to Lynn, and the feeling was mutual. The sense that we were becoming a couple was clear, and it was not just a fling or superficial encounter. I stayed with her often from then on, and we continued to experience a closeness that grew over time.

Lynn was financially secure and had a history of living well due to her family's financial success. She had been divorced for several years, and her ex-husband remained close to her and their kids. Her financial situation and mine were leagues apart, and I felt somewhat uncomfortable about the differences. It did not bother Lynn, and it never became an issue. In almost every other area except money, we got along well and decided to take the next step and get married.

As with almost all my marriages except the last, I wonder why getting married was the next step. We could have continued and been happy. Yet, we decided to take that next "till death do us part" step. We had a very informal wedding behind her house in California. It was very different from my large and formal wedding with Avis. Lynn studied to become a minister and was ordained. Her friend, also an ordained minister, conducted the simple unofficial ceremony attended by her children and mine where she lived near the beach in Los Angeles. I felt happy to be with her, and we enjoyed each other's company. Lynn was self-assured and mature. From the start, we had many good times together.

Not long after we were married, I developed Multiple Myeloma, a problematic form of cancer to treat and survive. I was fortunate to be in Boston, a city with some of the most advanced cancer clinics in the world. I underwent a stem cell replacement treatment, necessitating my being in an isolation room for several days because I had no white cells to protect me from infection. Lynn visited me in the hospital in the isolation room, and we could only talk through an intercom. I was almost always exhausted and could barely speak. She had to confront my treatment and the distinct possibility that I would not survive. Seeing me in the isolation room scared her and foreshadowed what she might have imagined as her future with me. It was too much for her. She realized she could not deal with the stress of my illness. She realized she needed to move on.

MULTIPLE MYELOMA AND ME

I escaped from death twice. In 2015, I was diagnosed with multiple myeloma. I had been feeling exhausted and unable to do much, which for me was unusual. My doctor recommended a battery of tests. When the labs came back, it showed that 90% of my bone marrow was taken over by cancer. It was a death sentence.

I immediately went to Beth Israel Hospital, which used the best cancer-fighting technology and medications. The cancer won the battle for my body, and I would die unless the remaining treatment, a stem cell transplant, succeeded.

I was placed in a 'clean' room since my body could not fight off any infection. The procedure starts by taking out as many stem cells as they can, which in my case was, I think, nine million from my blood, and storing them for treatment to make them cancer-free. I was then given a lethal dose of chemotherapy to kill any remaining cancer in my bone marrow cells. It made me very sick. Then, my treated and cancer-free stem cells were injected back into my body.

These 'clean' stem cells miraculously migrated into the bone marrow and started up a new cycle of cells from which I could live. In weeks, they produced all the cells I needed: white, red, and platelets that all started from the stem cells. I have been living off of these original stem cells and the cells they produce ever since my treatment. I have been, until recently, doing remarkably well. Thank goodness for stem cell science and the doctors and nurses who treated me. Their dedication and hard work have kept me alive.

That treatment, plus the incredible and sometimes experimental chemo meds, kept me alive for these past six years. My cancer, spreading into my bones, was halted, and without that treatment, I would not have lived to write these words.

When Lynn ended our relationship, I truly understood and appreciated that she could not continue to love and support me through this illness that might result in a short and painful death. Unlike my reaction to Vicky, I did not freak out, feeling that I had been abandoned once again, and the vows in sickness and health only applied to the health part. I resigned to my fate and decided I would never have unconditional love, that I was born alone and would die the same way. At the time, I did not know that I was about to finally meet my true love. We go from what feels like an ending to a new beginning. It's how we learn to keep hope alive and never say never.

KAREN

Karen is the most beautiful gift the universe has ever given me.

My mother was raised at a time when women were expected to be passive and supportive. She and I grew up in a culture where a woman knew her place, and anything her husband did was always right. Because of that and how my father behaved, I could never tell how much she felt fulfilled or safe. Was she ever really happy or secure? I wanted a much healthier relationship in my marriage.

My dilemma has always been that my previous marriages were less exciting, challenging, or rewarding than the medicine I was exploring and learning. No two days are the same in medicine. Every situation, case, illness, or patient is new and different. Marriage too often represented a comfortable daily sameness.

At this point in my life, after all my marriages, I was feeling successful, good about myself, and meeting my professional needs to be a competent doctor and psychiatrist. I thought I was light years away from the pull of the black hole of anger I had towards my father. Despite all that, I was still failing to meet my needs, to love and be loved. There was no balance in my life, and more importantly, unlike my medical training, there were no mentors in my personal life to whom I could turn for guidance. I was on my own, flying solo and feeling vulnerable and lonely.

I needed to find someone with whom to grow old. That search led me to women passing through my life instead of being with me for the rest of my life. The lines from Rainer Maria Rilke's *Letter to a Young Poet*, which I recalled by the pond, once again gave me pause: *"Live the questions now. Perhaps then, someday, far in the future, you will gradually, without even noticing it, live your way into the answer."* The break with Lynn turned out to be a lucky break because it led me to Karen, with whom I finally feel I am living the answer.

Ironically, I had almost decided to stop the online dating dance when I met Karen on JDate. She immediately impressed me by being very open, direct, and honest. A simple conversation can tell a lot about a person and is refreshing. It was a measure of our ability to have an open conversation. I learned about her life and dreams, how she handled a very challenging marriage, and the struggles and rewards of being a mother to three girls. Karen lived in Connecticut with her three daughters for most of her life. She had been in a difficult and loveless marriage that ended in divorce. Before our meeting, she had accepted the possibility that she would be alone for the rest of her life.

There are many subtle cues to a person's personality, and I registered most of them. I had a real sense that she was someone I wanted to be with. After we had been together for a year, I finally understood why I wanted to take the next step and become husband and wife. We had a small wedding in the back of her house, and her family provided a warm setting. I no longer have relatives except my children, so being with her family was very special.

You might ask why I got married again. The answer is simple. I beat my cancer into submission and had a few more years to live. Looking at those remaining years, I did not want them to be empty, devoid of being loved and loving in return. I was confident that Karen would love me unconditionally to the very end. And this time, being in my late 70s, the odds of finally getting a happy ending were definitely in my favor.

Karen is seventeen years younger than I am. When we eventually talked about getting married, we looked at our age difference and my illness, and all she could say was, "At least I will have love in my life." And she does. I genuinely love Karen and am happier than I have ever been in my life. We, indeed, are partners.

We have a deep and abiding friendship that is very solid. In all the important ways, I feel profoundly close to Karen, deeper than I have ever experienced; I understand who she is, and she understands me. My relationship with Karen is the best relationship I have ever been in. Ironically, the best relationship is based on a mutual understanding of each other's best and worst selves. She once said to me, after we had been together for a few years, that I am the only man who sees her essence. She sees mine as well. I feel fortunate and have worked to finally change and grow up.

I have come to a place where a woman's confidence, intelligence, and sense of humor are more important than anything else. Except for my kids and some rare friends still alive, no one else would have totally accepted and loved me as much as Karen.

The qualities I value most in a relationship are evident in my relationship with Karen, and I feel it daily. What contributes to my happiness is a feeling that I love her, care about her, and want her to be happy. It feels like the same kind of emotions I have for my kids. She has many of the qualities I most prize in a relationship. She is very smart, self-confident, and usually able to find the right thing to do regardless of the circumstances. She quickly understands other people's points of view and somehow intuits their deeper feelings. That is so important. I only hope I live long enough to give her as many years of happiness as possible.

My time here may be short; my cancer has been under control for years, but Not anymore. My health has always been a concern with Karen. Despite everything, she is the only one who offers me unconditional love. I do the same for her. As I write these words, I face the inevitable unless something changes dramatically. I am deeply saddened by the prospect of dying and not ever being able to know how those I love are doing. It makes my time with them all the more precious.

OUR TIME IS UP

At the end of a session, I would often have to say, "Our time is up." In many ways, that is an appropriate way to end this book. Our time together is up, and after 85 years, as my cancer tries to win the battle, my time may also be up. These are supposed to be my golden years, yet darkness constantly hovers around the edges.

As I wrote this story about myself, I felt like I was looking into a mirror that showed my past, present, and perhaps future. Even now, it isn't easy to understand why I made many of my choices and how lucky I was to connect with some amazing people from whom I learned so much. I can look over these pages and see many decisions and transformations that brought me to this last chapter. Reading it, I feel a tightness in my chest and a mix of emotions. I can read about myself, but I still need to do more work to fully understand why I made the decisions that became turning points and transformations in my life. I have become the patient to myself as the therapist.

It feels strange to hold 85 years' worth of space and time in my hands, condensed into a book about my life. I'm not just telling this story; I lived it. Reading these words feels surreal. My life seems to fly by in each episode. It is my life from the beginning to what may be the end. I can only conclude that you can't write a memoir when you are young.

So here we are now. I hope you find this story of my life

as helpful to you as it has been to me. When I write the words "Our time is up," it's very real for me, and not just more words on the page.

The end ... is not yet written.